How Higher-Ed Leaders Derail:

A Survival Guide for Leaders

———————

PATRICK SANAGHAN

with

JILLIAN LOHNDORF

———————

ACADEMIC IMPRESSIONS | 2018
DENVER, CO

Published by Academic Impressions.

CR Mrig Company. 4601 DTC Blvd., Suite 800, Denver, CO 80237.

For reproduction, distribution, or copy permissions, or to order additional copies, please contact the Academic Impressions office at 720.488.6800 or visit:

http://bit.ly/2qbHuLr

Academic Impressions

ISBN: 978-1-948658-02-7

Printed in the United States of America.

CONTENTS

1 FOREWORD

1 The Peril of Smartship

9 CHAPTER 1 - STEPS TO IDENTIFYING AND PREVENTING DERAILMENT

9 Overview

10 How to Identify Derailment

22 How to Prevent Derailment

43 Summary

51 CHAPTER 2 - THE SEDUCTION OF THE LEADER: A DYNAMIC TO AVOID

51 Overview

52 What Does *Seduction of the Leader* Look Like?

59 How Does *Seduction of the Leader* Occur?

63 What Are the Underlying Dynamics of *Seduction of the Leader?*

67 What Are the Structural Elements of *Seduction of the Leader?*

70 Proven Strategies to Counter *Seduction of the Leader*

87 Closing Thoughts

89 CHAPTER 3 - MICROMANAGEMENT—IS IT INCURABLE?

89 Overview

90 What Does a Micromanager Look Like?

93 The Negative Impact of Micromanagers

97   Advice for Dealing with a Micromanaging Boss

103   Advice for Micromanagers

111   An Informal Micromanagement Assessment

118   CHAPTER 4 – THE IGNORANCE OF ARROGANCE

118   Overview

119   What Does Arrogance Look Like?

124   The Impact of the Arrogant Leader

134   Strategies to Adopt When Faced with an Arrogant Leader

153   An Informal Arrogance Self-Assessment

158   Summary

163   APPENDIX: SUPERVISORY DIALOGUE

163   Overview

167   A Proposed Model

173   The Rationale Behind the 7 Supervisory Questions

180   Summary

181   ABOUT THE AUTHOR

FOREWORD

by Pat Sanaghan, Amit Mrig, and Daniel Fusch

Leadership matters; rarely has it mattered more. Facing enrollment, financial, and other challenges, institutions need creative, courageous, and effective people throughout their middle management and executive roles. In many ways, the challenges facing institutional leaders are similar to the challenges famed explorers Lewis and Clark encountered during their expedition across the Western half of the United States. Today's leaders are traversing unknown territory without a map and are racing against the clock.

When we lead in the absence of a map, often we rely too heavily on what we already know or think we know well. We fall back on tradition, losing sight of the creativity and the risks we need to take now. We rely more heavily on "smartship" than leadership. This is a tendency we see in organizations across all industries, but we are especially prone to it in higher education because of the unique weight we assign to hierarchy and tradition.

The Peril of Smartship

In higher ed, there is a widely-held myth that the smartest person in the room should lead. Therefore, we often take for granted that someone who is smart *can* lead, and we don't take steps to develop or prepare our people for leadership positions. Many mid-career leaders in academia are placed in leadership positions too quickly and without adequate support. They may rely too heavily on a mentor, or freeze in the face of difficult decisions, finding themselves in over their heads, and find themselves isolated and derailing.

All leaders are smart, but not all smart people are leaders. Too much focus on IQ and not enough on EQ (emotional intelligence) creates the conditions for toxic leadership. Things are moving too fast and are too complex for one person to figure it out, no matter how smart. Effective leaders trust their people, convene appropriate stakeholders to help make sense of the path ahead, and seek regular and open feedback. There is a humility and creativity needed in leadership, especially in an industry changing as rapidly as higher education.

The emphasis on how smart someone is vs. how effective they are as a *leader* is especially pervasive in higher education, which as an industry is:

1. characterized by formality and hierarchy

2. highly focused on credentials

3. not good at asking for help

4. risk averse

These characteristics of higher-ed institutions make leadership in this sector both different and difficult, fostering four leadership dynamics that are especially hard to identify, address, and resolve in an academic setting: *derailment, seduction of the leader, arrogant leadership,* and *micromanagement.*

The Formality of Higher Ed

Higher education's emphasis on position, formality, and hierarchy can create an organizational culture in a college or university where those with less power and influence often have great difficulty communicating anything but positive or benign information to those who have more power and influence. The hierarchies in postsecondary institutions prevent information from flowing up swiftly from the front lines to the leader. And the concern with titles, ceremony, and proper decorum creates barriers between different levels in the institution. "Madame President, "Mr. President," "Madame Provost" … The expectations around respectful and formal communication and the difficulty in approaching leaders with open and candid feedback can foster a "seduction of the leader" dynamic, in which leaders do not receive accurate and timely intel about how matters actually are. This in turn stalls quick action and decisive decision making.

Junior faculty and staff especially may have difficulty sharing honest feedback or contrary views to those voiced by more senior staff or tenured faculty. But as these junior employees are often those interacting most often with students, they have critical and necessary intel to share. Yet the formality of higher education means that their opinion carries little weight and leaders rarely include them in departmental meetings or proactively seek their input.

Leaders in the higher education environment often lack the awareness of this dynamic that they need in order to subvert it. As a result, *the seduction of the leader* occurs; leaders swiftly get surrounded by either sycophants or by competent employees who believe their opinions to be unwelcome and consequently do not share them. Seduced into believing matters are going much more smoothly than they actually are, leaders often learn about and have the opportunity to respond to issues and new challenges far too late.

Emphasis on Credentials

The very elements that make academia strong also make it vulnerable. In higher education, enormous emphasis is placed on individual intellectual achievement, credentials, and skeptical thinking. Academics are incentivized to publish, to be declarative in their assertions, and to approach change or alternate views with skepticism. "Being right" matters—a lot.

An academic with impressive credentials and publications can move up the ranks quickly in one area of the institution, but this career path doesn't provide a "view from the balcony" or a holistic perspective on the institution and its efforts. This makes it difficult both to develop a coherent vision of the future for their department, division, or college—and to organize and lead efforts across units.

The qualities that make for a distinguished researcher or scholar don't often translate to being a good leader. Higher ed prioritizes and incentivizes individual achievement over team achievement. But leadership is a team sport, not an individual one. The emphasis on individual, intellectual achievement in higher ed creates an environment in which arrogant (or seemingly arrogant) leaders can thrive for a time.

But the traits exhibited by arrogant leaders are exactly the traits we *don't* need if institutions are going to confront the complex challenges facing them and both survive and thrive in the years ahead. Highly credentialed but ineffective leaders often fail to listen to their colleagues and to seek fresh perspectives; they may believe they already understand the landscape fully and have all the answers. In turn, colleagues stop participating in meetings and discussions, believing their contributions will not be valued or received well.

This creates a toxic dynamic. We need leaders instead who can set their ego aside and seek input from others—leaders who recognize that they have only one perspective and that by themselves, they have only limited access to information. Ron Heifetz writes that most leaders "die with their mouths open," meaning that we talk too much and listen too little, forgetting that we are each equipped with two ears and only one mouth.

Not Good at Asking for Help

Leaders frequently derail in higher education, crashing mid-career and failing to live up to the potential they were assumed to have. Even college presidencies frequently crash; the turnover at the top can be daunting to read about or experience. And one of the ten leading reasons why presidents and leaders at all levels of the organization derail is that they fail to ask for help.

There is a myth pervasive in higher education that asking for help shows indecision, incompetence, or weakness— that a leader should already know everything they need to know to move forward and navigate the complexities of their position. When leaders, especially new leaders, finally reach out for help and advice, it is often too late.

The irony is that in higher education, perhaps more than any other industry, help is readily available. The collegial nature of most college campuses means that most leaders have access to colleagues or staff who would gladly provide support and assistance—if asked.

Additionally, when a leader *does* ask questions in this collegial environment, this builds trust and shared invest-ment in the work ahead. Asking questions conveys curiosity and interest, and—counterintuitively—conveys to others that you are smart, that you are engaged in learning and in seeking the best possible answers. Conversely, when a leader doesn't ask questions, others begin to resent the apparent arrogance of the leader (who, they suspect, thinks he/she knows all the answers) and to doubt their discernment and judgment. Losing faith in the leader, they become less likely to offer help and more likely to doubt the leader's decisions.

Risk Aversion

Academia and the promise of tenure often attracts individuals who are risk averse, and the cultures of academic departments rarely reward risk taking. The Ph.D. program, the dissertation, the "publish or perish" drive toward tenure—these are all endeavors that place enormous pressures on young academics, and the processes by which they advance in their field and career are unforgiving of mistakes or failures. It often appears better to play it safe, knowing your one particular area very deeply and well, rather than attempting genuinely novel research. As a consequence, mid-level academic leaders who progress up the ranks from the faculty often lack a history of failing and learning from failure. Rather than being encouraged to take productive risks and learn from the results, academic leaders are trained to not make mistakes.

Yet risk taking is critical to effective leadership, especially in times when complex challenges require complex and innovative solutions. Risk-averse leaders focus on preventing things from going wrong and are less likely to pursue things that might go right, especially if the path there is uncharted and ambiguous, and the outcome is not yet certain. This type of organizational culture fosters inaction and creates the conditions in which micro-management—one of the most damaging leadership dynamics—surfaces and thrives.

Motivated by fear of failure or public embarrassment, or of being left out of the information loop, micromanagers strive to control their people and processes. They value order rather than innovation and predictability rather than risk. This is a leadership dynamic that not only creates toxic work environments but holds departments back from trying new things and improving. When you're moving quickly, you have to empower your people to be creative, to pilot and iterate and learn quickly, and to risk failure in the service of finding the best available paths forward. People have to be trusted and incentivized to push in their own direction. In this environment, the leader is not "in control," and the leader doesn't have all the answers; they have to rely on the autonomy, perspective, and improvisation of their colleagues.

The risk aversion that is endemic in many institutions of higher education throttles this kind of entrepreneurial, learning culture, choking it before it can really grow. Micromanaging leaders often thrive and retain their positions because they operate as guardians of the status quo.

Conclusion

Drawing on decades of experience working closely and consulting with leaders at every level of higher education, this book will explore these four dynamics in depth: *derailment, seduction of the leader, arrogant leadership,* and *micromanagement.* These dynamics are persistent and pervasive in higher education; yet they are rarely discussed or addressed. They need to be; that is why we believe this book is necessary and timely.

Each chapter will unpack the causes and challenges unique to one of these four dynamics—and will offer practical strategies and real solutions to these difficult problems.

The appendix at the end of the book will present a model for conducting a healthy supervisory dialogue. When adopted within a department, unit, or institution, this kind of dialogue builds healthy and empowering partnerships between leaders and their teams, and helps prevent many of the dysfunctional leadership dynamics we will discuss in this book.

We hope you will find this book useful, and use it to grow your own capacity as a leader in your higher-ed career.

CHAPTER 1 STEPS TO IDENTIFYING & PREVENTING DERAILMENT

Overview

Across sectors, it is estimated that upwards of 50% of all leaders and managers fail. The costs of leadership derailment are high, especially when this happens to a senior leader: financial costs, as well as the intangibles of the negative impact on organizational culture, morale, and effectiveness.

With so much at stake, why is it that so many leaders fail? And why aren't more people talking about it? Derailment often remains a taboo topic, discussed behind closed doors.

While the Center for Creative Leadership (C.C.L.) has been one of the research pioneers in the field of leadership derailment for several decades, much of the current research on derailment focuses on the corporate sector—although derailment is also alive and well in higher education. Just as in the corporate world, leadership derailment in higher education occurs when a "youngish" (30-40 years), high-performing, and promising leader unravels and their career becomes undone due to inappropriate and ineffective behaviors. They are either fired outright or demoted, or their career fizzles out slowly as they hit a leadership plateau that they never recover from. The promise and potential hit a wall.

The good news is that derailment leaves clues; it doesn't just happen overnight. There are distinct behavioral signs that can predict derailment, even if they are often ignored. Often, it's hoped that the ineffective behaviors will magically disappear or that the leader will simply get better over time, perhaps due to maturity or experience.

However, the reality is that leaders tend to get worse without intervention. While the odds of improvement are small, the opportunity exists.

While the dynamics of *presidential* derailment are separate (and addressed specifically in "Preventing Presidential Derailment," available at www.academicimpressions.com/preventing-presidential-derailment), derailment can affect the entirety of campus leadership. Avoiding it starts with a conversation among campus leaders to understand the complexities embedded in this leadership dynamic. It involves looking directly into the issues and behaviors at the heart of derailment.

How to Identify Derailment

Basically - setting the stage: cautions; what not to do

"The Mythology of High Potentials"

High potential employees or "HI Po's" are a term that human resources and talent management professionals use to describe the top 5% or so of performers who have the talent and skills to move up the career ladder and make a powerful contribution to an organization's success. The corporate sector uses this term rampantly, and has

Why this? Seems odd to focus on this? Better approach would be to advance all who aspire to leadership position mechanisms in place to develop their skill sets and grow their leadership skills, including job rotations, "stretch" assignments, mentor programs, and high profile leadership programs. They invest resources in Hi-Po's with the hope that it will pay off sometime in the future.

While higher education may not use the same term or processes, Hi-Po's certainly exist on many campuses, and Hi-Po's are especially susceptible to the derailment syndrome. The Hi-Po identification and selection process is very predictable and many of these high potentials look and act the same. It can be described as, "I am not sure what it is, but they just look like leaders to me."

- They have a fair amount of "charisma," which is what gets them noticed.

- They are ambitious and make it known. They reach out for assignments, "volunteer" to lead a group, team or task force, etc.

- They are quick on their feet, able to articulately answer questions in the moment. What impresses people is not the quality of the answer, but the speed in which they respond.

- They tend to be attractive physically or they have a physical "presence," which helps them stand out from the crowd.

Hi-Po's also have many positive traits, such as a strong work ethic, persistence, resilience, and a "can do" attitude. Higher education needs as many high performers as possible, but should be careful in the selection process. The *"they just look like a leader to me"* approach can lead to selecting folks that look good but cannot lead. Their leadership deficiencies can be difficult to catch in time, ending in derailment.

The Telltale Signs of Derailers: Failure Leaves Clues

Over-Reliance on a Sponsor or Patron

Often a senior leader takes a shine to an assertive, task-focused young leader who produces results fast. This initial appeal can become a protective cocoon which insulates the emerging leader when they start to hit some bumps. The young leader doesn't develop their skills simply because they don't have to. Unfortunately, such protection does not last forever, and when the senior leader moves on, the young leader, and their limitations, are exposed. They do not have the skills to lead others when their guardian leaves.

CASE STUDY: THE SHADOW OF THE SPONSOR

Several years ago, I worked with a President and his senior team, who had a derailing leader. The young leader was the newly appointed CFO, named "Paul," who wanted to make a splash early and fast. He'd had some early career success regarding finances, and saw himself as a change agent. He was also a favorite of the president—which everyone knew, including Paul.

Unfortunately, he couldn't connect with any of the cabinet members and constantly complained about the "old boys" network. In his effort to lobby for the areas he was in charge of, he failed to develop a systemic view of the campus. He wanted to make things happen, but they just weren't, and in his frustration became aggressive in meetings, discourteous to others, and couldn't keep commitments.

The Shadow of the Sponsor, continued

The president offered excuses for his behavior by saying, "He is trying to create a sense of excellence" or "He has very high standards for himself and others," but lots of people got bruised along the way. Paul's colleagues all agreed that he was quite smart and had a great work ethic, but they found it very difficult to work with him for a host of reasons. It boiled down to the fact that they didn't trust him, his intentions, or his aspirations. They did not like the way he treated people, and it seemed that he was "allowed" to behave in ways that were inappropriate given the campus's collegial culture. A yearly employee engagement survey conducted by the VP of Human Resources showed the scores for most divisions were quite positive, but unfortunately, Paul's division's scores were abysmal. This validated survey created a plain, data-based picture of a division in deep trouble.

I wanted to understand his perspective about the situation and went into the conversation both eager and curious. I was struck by several things: Paul was a terrible listener and talked at me most of the time; he took no ownership for the data at all and communicated that a few disgruntled employees had "poisoned the well." I mentioned that this divisional survey included almost 100 people, so I found it difficult to see how a handful of people could produce such dismal results with a validated instrument. He simply ignored my comment. He had an astonishingly positive perception of himself and belittled those who didn't "get it."

I then met with the President to share my findings. He insisted that Paul could be successful, if people would just move forward and start supporting him. I strongly disagreed with his perspective.

The Shadow of the Sponsor, continued

I shared some information that I received from the Vice President of Human Resources: Paul's division had almost 90% turnover in the first year. Good people fled and sought other positions throughout the campus, or left the institution for other campuses. The president argued that there was a lot of dead wood in that division and Paul was doing the tough work needed to achieve excellence. However, what he didn't know was that Paul was now on his second cadre of people, all selected by Paul, who were beginning to leave the division. It was a toxic environment, and everyone on campus knew this.

Paul lasted one more year, during which time two Vice Presidents resigned, and the Board got involved in the situation. It took over a year to find an appropriate replacement for him, because the word on the street was the division was dysfunctional and damaged.

The campus learned valuable lessons about the price that people pay for the little that derailers contribute. If the President had better listened to the information he received, and communicated in strong and clear terms that Paul's kind of leadership was not effective or wanted, the situation might have been salvageable. But his fondness for Paul got in the way of doing the right thing and communicated to everyone on campus that certain people could get away with that kind of negative leadership.

Things to watch for in any leader — existing or emerging

Arrogance: The Mother of all Derailers

Tim Irwin explains this in his excellent book *Derailed: Five Lessons Learned from Catastrophic Failures of Leadership*, accurately identifying one of the pervasive flaws that derailers possess. Other researchers, too, have highlighted arrogance as a "fatal flaw."

As Irwin explains, "Arrogance is a career killer." Higher education has its fair share of arrogant leaders who believe they are smarter than everyone else. They suck the air out of every conversation they have, seem to know everything, and are closed to other's perspectives or honest feedback about their own ideas and leadership effectiveness.

Arrogance isn't quiet or subtle; it's as obvious as a cold blast of air and equally distasteful. When interviewing new people, hiring managers need to pay attention to behaviors such as:

- Interrupting.

- Not asking any questions (because arrogant people already know the answers).

- Providing simple and "obvious" solutions to complex and thorny issues.

- Talking way too much for way too long (arrogant people are horrible listeners).

- Talking a lot about themselves, their accomplishments and how they have added value to their organizations.

These same behaviors should be kept in mind when considering people for promotions. It is a good idea to seek feedback from current coworkers; they may have a plethora of stories, anecdotes, and distasteful experiences to share.

For more information on leadership arrogance—and how to defuse it or navigate around it—see Chapter 4, later in this book.

A Lack of Integrity

Integrity is the keystone of personal trust and leadership withers without it. This lack is one of the most serious fatal flaws of derailers. If people experience or even perceive that a leader lacks integrity, that leader will fail.

The reality is that derailers are mostly out for themselves and often use others to get ahead. They have an acute sense of organizational politics and seek out others in positions of power and influence to ingratiate themselves, take on assignments to help pad their resume, and take courses and programs to punch their own ticket. They take more credit than is due, and speak up when senior leadership is in the room to impress, but contribute little to collaborative efforts overall. Outward appearances are important to them; as long as they "look good," that is all that matters.

Because they are often talented and have a strong technical and/or functional skillset, derailing leaders often advance quickly, early in their career. This fuels their appetite to continue to move up the ladder in quest of higher positions, compensation, and recognition. Unfortunately, they do not learn much outside of their circle of competence and don't develop other skills and qualities that would make them more effective leaders. People know who these individuals are and their reputation precedes them. As their career develops, the challenges and assignments get more complex, and they need help in order to be successful. Unfortunately, the word on the street is very accurate, and people have no motivation to help someone who is only out for themselves, even if it would benefit the organization.

This lack of integrity can manifest in several ways:

- **Shifting blame** onto others when things start to go wrong and mistakes begin to emerge. They demonstrate a lack of responsibility for their flaws and a propensity to point the finger at others.

- **An inability to go the "last mile,"** instead leaving important work unfinished. This is often due to poor attention to detail, often glossing over things instead of putting in the real time and attention that is needed to do things right. This creates a perception of undependability, making them untrustworthy.

- **An inability to keep their word** and commitments, replaced with elaborate excuses for why things didn't get done. If confronted about their lack of performance, they often lie outright, which communicates that they can't be trusted.

Strengths Become Weaknesses

Derailing leaders frequently can be quite charismatic and personable. They have strong social skills and often can relate well to others when they want to. However, this charm and charisma is often inauthentic and in service of their personal agendas. They scan the room while talking to someone, looking for someone influential to impress, or are nice only when they need something. Their lack of self-awareness about how they come across to others is startling at times. They simply do not see how unflatteringly their colleagues perceive them.

They also often have strong technical or functional skills (e.g., finance, legal, technology, and project management), which helps create some initial career success. They can contribute quickly, solve problems and make things happen. If they have an assertive personality, the combination of technical skills and a forceful approach can be a powerful mixture, which creates a "can do" reputation. Senior leaders appreciate these types of folks. They will provide those who do with support and resources and even political cover. Unfortunately, technical and functional skillsets become less important as one moves up the organizational ladder. Sophisticated abilities like strategic thinking, systems thinking, adaptive change management, and understanding complex campus politics become more important to a leader's success. Political cover hides a limited skill set as the young leader advances upward. Over time, there is little motivation to change their behavior or expand their portfolio as they solidify an "It's working, why change now?" attitude.

The combination of protectionism and too-quick promotion means that when they are placed into a higher leadership role that demands a more robust skillset; their limited repertoire is simply not enough to lead others. This can be hard to see. Instead of understanding how what got them to where they are is holding them back, they tend to double their efforts in a vain attempt to assert their leadership and gain control. This results in ineffective behaviors like micromanaging, excluding others, working excessive hours, and limiting communication. They isolate themselves and others as more volatile behaviors begin to emerge. Derailers often have great difficulty relating *authentically* to others, due to their lack of insight and emotional intelligence. Their inability to understand their impact on others means they are insensitive to the needs of others and can be abrasive, bullying, and volatile, especially under stress. Their erratic behaviors can emerge without warning or apparent reason. In many places, there is a pervasive mentality where people who produce results are forgiven for inappropriate behaviors. However, this mindset is as much a hindrance to the individual as it is to the institution. As their behaviors become more well-known, people start avoiding working with them, and they get quietly cut off from the mainstream of campus life. Their inability to connect with others, build trust, and share successes, prevents them from building the *relational capital* necessary to work effectively with others. In the collegial nature of higher education, positive relationships are vital to a leader's success. Without relational capital, a leader simply cannot achieve meaningful things in service of the institution's vision and goals.

As Kaiser & Kaplan explain in *Fear Your Strengths*, "The stronger the strength, the greater danger of taking it too far." In the end, what got a derailing leader to their new leadership role isn't enough to keep them there. This can play out in a variety of ways:

- "Visionaries" become unrealistic dreamers who fall in love with every creative possibility they encounter.

- An "action-oriented" leader becomes a mean autocrat, bruising people along the way and insisting that things be done their way or not at all.

- A "decisive" leader makes a string of bad decisions because they have not thought through the potential impacts and implications of their decisions. They gauge their success by how *many* decisions they make, not on how good they are.

- A "collaborative" leader tries to include everyone in everything and nothing meaningful is accomplished.

- An "optimistic" leader convinces themselves that everything will be all right, despite powerful evidence that a crisis is looming, and the time for proactive behaviors are missed.

[handwritten margin note: ignor crises]

Kaiser & Kaplan explain that a developmental approach focused exclusively on a leader's strengths will not prevent derailment. Every leader needs to be committed to continual learning and development, in order to avoid developing an over-reliance on their strengths, or under-developing their weaknesses. They need to know and own their strengths, and deeply understand their weaknesses, in order to grow. For too many years, leadership development was a "deficit" model which worked primarily on improving a leader's weaknesses. Several best sellers have captured a great deal of attention and refocused much of the leadership research on leaders' strengths vs. their weaknesses, including *Now Discover Your Strengths* (2001) by Marcus Buckingham and Donald O. Sutton and *Strengths Finders 2.0* (2007) by Tom Roth. These books explain that having a full picture of their capacities, limitations, and skills creates a choice point for young leaders. They might not decide to improve their weaknesses, but at least they have the opportunity to choose.

Inability to Build a Team

To build and nurture a team is a daunting task and is a prerequisite for leadership in higher education. Effective leaders get things done through the great effort of others, while derailing leaders simply do not have what it takes to create a high performing team. They lack the social skills (e.g., good listening, emotional composure, sensitivity to other's needs, sharing credit and recognition, etc.) absolutely necessary for a team leader. They have difficulty molding a team for several reasons:

- They often have an autocratic leadership style, especially under stress, which translates into an "It's my way or the highway" attitude.

- They tend to avoid conflict. However, conflict doesn't get better with age. It takes real courage *and* skill to effectively deal with team conflict.

- They can be abrasive and bullying when confronted with contrary opinions, ideas, facts, or scenarios. Others shut down in their presence because they quickly realize that they will not be heard.

- In recruiting team members, they frequently choose mediocre talent or "comfortable cloning" where they pick people who are similar to them in background, temperament, education, etc., and who are therefore "comfortable" to them. They rarely seek out diversity, because they see differences as liabilities instead of assets.

In the fast paced world of higher education, full of complexity and ambiguity, we will need effective teams throughout our campuses collaboratively working together. Derailers simply won't be able to function in that kind of environment.

Higher education is facing many complex challenges, and derailers tend to find change and transitions especially difficult to deal with. They often get trapped in their offices instead of proactively interacting with others. They can become perfectionistic, over-analyzing everything, which can delay decision-making. They lose sight of the bigger picture and focus on minute details. If they are part of an organizational redesign and find themselves reporting to new leaders, working with new people and dealing with a different institutiona culture, they often cannot make the adjustment. Under times of stress and change, a derailing leader's inappropriate and ineffective behaviors begin to emerge, and their need for control can quickly develop into micromanaging others. The pace of derailment quickens under these circumstances, and there are very few ways to prevent or even slow down the derailment process.

Failure to Meet Long-Term Goals

When a derailing leader starts to miss deadlines, under-performs regarding agreed-upon goals, and becomes a liability within a work group, the damage has already begun. Instead of reaching out to their peers and supervisors and seeking support and advice, they tend to isolate themselves, withdraw into their offices, and start to micromanage their direct reports.

It is difficult for them to understand why they are failing, after experiencing initial success in their careers and often after performing at high levels. What worked before simply doesn't work now, and their weaknesses outshine their limited strengths—and everyone knows it.

This is why effective supervision is so essential to building and supporting leaders on campus. A derailing leader rarely asks for help, so missing deadlines and agreed-upon goals is an early warning system for a supervisor. Supervisors need to intervene quickly to assess the situation.

How to Prevent Derailment

There are two ways to approach derailment: *personally* and *institutionally*. Both are needed in equal measure.

Personal Strategies for Preventing Derailment

In Chapter 2 of this book, I will discuss how critical it is that leaders regularly **seek honest feedback**. The best leaders actively seek anonymous feedback from others. They understand that even though most people are open and honest individuals, they will rarely "tell it like it is" to their leaders, *even if they are asked*, for a host of reasons: people have a hard time delivering difficult news; the "collegial" nature of higher education tends to be conflict averse; avoidance of hurt feelings; etc. Therefore, leaders need to be proactive when it comes to obtaining feedback from others:

1. Engage in a 360° Feedback Process

The 360° process is a performance-feedback approach that has been around for decades. When conducted well, it is one of the most powerful and insightful learning experiences a leader can undertake. In this well-organized process, you'll solicit anonymous feedback about your strengths and the areas in which you need development from multiple stakeholders (such as peers, direct reports, and customers). The process takes real courage, but we have found it well worth the risk.

That said, the process is somewhat complicated, so it's important to do your homework before you undertake this learning process. We suggest the following two resources, which offer helpful guidance: *What Is 360 Degree Feedback?* by Mark Miller (Kindle edition, 2012), and *The Art and Science of 360 Degree Feedback* by Richard Lepsinger and Anntoinette D. Lucia (print and Kindle editions, 2009).

In short, the 360° process involves soliciting (anonymous) feedback from a diverse set of stakeholders who interact with a particular leader. The primary purpose is to create an honest and holistic picture about how a particular individual is seen and experienced by people they work with.

A confidential report is created after participants provide the necessary information, detailing the strengths and weaknesses of the individual. Most importantly, the supervisor needs to help create an action plan that builds on the strength of the individual and improves the areas of needed development. This is essential. A 360° feedback process is not an intellectual exercise. It is meant to create a rich database that moves an individual toward change and enhancement.

Ideally, leaders should participate in this 360° feedback process yearly. Some attention needs to be paid to the process so it doesn't become a routine exercise but instead creates opportunity for the development of leadership skills throughout the organization.

We also recommend that you apply the 360° process to yourself and to others—not to yourself alone. Doing it only for yourself might convey an unintended message that you are in trouble. The process is optimal when it's done yearly, as a built-in component of a team's standard operating procedure. In addition to generating information about how others see you as a leader, feedback processes communicate to others that you value others' opinions, are open to learning, and are committed to increasing your self-awareness. These are all powerful messages to convey.

Most human resources (HR) departments can support and coordinate a 360° feedback process to ensure quality and anonymity. It is essential that the people providing feedback do so anonymously. This ensures honesty. If you don't have a well-run HR department or the organizational capacity to conduct a 360° process, our next strategy will be helpful to you.

2. Conduct a *Leadership Audit*

The 360° feedback process is robust and involves a validated instrument; the *leadership audit* is a lighter version. It's a tool we created a few years ago, and you can read a full explanation of it on pages 71-74. Here is a quick, informal version that you can use at any time. In this version, the leader asks three simple questions that will provide them with helpful, qualitative information:

A. What are my five greatest strengths as a leader?

B. What is one area of needed development I should be aware of and conscious about?

C. What is one piece of advice you would like to provide me that would help me in my current role?

Don't be fooled by the simplicity of these questions; they will reap powerful information.

It is most helpful to select at least 10 people to participate in this process including peers, supervisors, subordinates, and coworkers. Anonymity is essential, so it is often helpful for the human resources department or another trusted leader to collect the data and create a confidential report for review.

After that, the leader who undertakes the *leadership audit* can meet with their direct supervisor and share in broad strokes the major themes that emerged from the audit. This is their decision to make. No one should ever feel like they *should* share all their data with their direct supervisor. (This goes for the 360° feedback process, as well.) These feedback processes are learning tools to enhance the leader's effectiveness and should not be part of an "official" performance review process.

3. Cultivate Confidants

Where do leaders, especially presidents, go when they are dealing with their leadership challenges, doubts, and fears? Heifetz and Linsky suggest they find at least two "confidants" who are deeply trusted and honest individuals who will provide constructive feedback, advice, and wise council, and develop an ongoing relationship. These are authentic allies who will listen carefully, push back on ideas, help develop insight, and act as sanctuaries when the inevitable storms hit. They are invaluable. A young leader should be meeting with their confidants on a regular basis, not only in times of trouble. No leader should ever walk alone.

4. Build in Introspection

It's helpful for leaders to keep some kind of journal or record of their thoughts and feelings as they lead others. This reflective discipline is not easy to do, yet it creates the opportunity for deep learning and develops self-awareness. There are plenty of ways to capture your reflections and thoughts: a paper journal, recording or video, or a note-taking app. Those who can't "find the time" for this simple practice might already be in trouble. Derailing leaders often lack self-awareness and simply fail to reflect on their behaviors, feelings and leadership effectiveness. Capturing these thoughts will often reveal important and strategic information that might not be apparent at first glance. Some thoughtful questions can create the framework for thinking about leadership effectiveness:

- What challenges am I encountering?

- What questions seem to come up over and over?

- Who confides in me? Asks me for advice?

- What is the "pulse" of my team? How are they feeling? How are they performing?

- Are my team meetings productive? How do I know this?

- Who are my allies? Who can I confide in?

- What is the quality of my important decisions recently?

- What doubts am I having? What makes me anxious?

- What is going well? What do I need to be appreciative of?

- Who do I need to recognize and appreciate more?

- What are other leaders in my organization talking about? Worried about? Excited about?

- Can people provide me with honest feedback?

5. Broaden the Professional Portfolio

Proactively avoid becoming a one trick pony with a narrow skillset by taking on "stretch" assignments that will build leadership strengths. Consciously choose new tasks that focus on learning new things, without being too big, complex, or difficult. Confidants and supervisors can provide honest advice about the nature and complexity of stretch assignments and provide emotional support as the learning curve deepens.

Leaders should invest in their own professional development in a conscious and disciplined way through a

Learning Agenda that identifies: books they will read, courses they will take, programs they will attend, as well as people they want to learn from and potential mentors.

6. Get an Executive Coach

Executive coaching has been widely used in the corporate sector for years to help leaders be more effective, and is beginning to become a more familiar practice in higher education. It is primarily a skill-based support process and is not therapy. In a Harvard Business Review article, *What Can Coaching Do for You?* (2009), Diane Coutu and Carol Kaufman identify the 3 main reasons coaches are utilized in organizations, in order of priority:

A. Develop high potential leaders or facilitate a leadership transition.

B. Act as a sounding board.

C. Address derailing behavior.

There are many variations in how coaching is done. Some coaches work only face to face, while others work on the phone or use videoconferencing tools, such as Skype. Some coaches will collect data about the "coachee" through surveys and interviews, while others will work only with the client's own identification of needs. Regardless of the methodology, the coaching process generally looks like this:

- Identifying the coachee's challenge.

- Identifying specific coaching goals that will address the challenge.

- Understanding the challenge in light of self–assessment.

- Creating and brainstorming strategies to achieve goals.

- Acting upon those strategies.

- Tracking the success of the strategies, both the tangible outcomes and the client's subjective experience.

- Acknowledge successes.

- Evaluating the coaching process.

Suggested Resources

A couple of suggestions for people who are interested in finding more about coaching:

Coaching for Breakthrough Success (2013). Jack Canfield and Peter Chee provide some very helpful ideas about coaching and have a holistic perspective about coaching that some will find interesting. They believe that coaching is an empowering process of drawing out solutions from people through effective listening and asking great questions.

Thanks for the Feedback (2014). Douglass Stone and Sheila Heen have an interesting take on how to receive feedback from others, whether through coaching, working with peers or in a supervisory process. They identify 3 different kinds of feedback: 1) Appreciation, 2) Coaching, 3) Evaluation, which are very different processes. They also suggest strategies on how to utilize the feedback you receive in the most constructive way possible.

Creating Coaching Cultures: What Business Leaders Expect and How to Get There (2009). This Center for Creative Leadership white paper identifies some of the essential elements of an organizational or "systems" approach to coaching.

CONNECT WITH THE BEST EXECUTIVE COACHES

Executive Coaching with Academic Impressions can help you gain clarity in your career and reach your full potential. We are focused on working with high-performing leaders to increase their level of self-awareness and hone their skillset. Executive coaches are critical companions in this developmental process and Academic Impressions is thrilled to be working with amazing coaches who each have experience in higher education.

You can learn more about Executive Coaching at:

https://www.academicimpressions.com/execu tive-coaching/

---

7. Learn to Ask for Help

There is a pervasive myth that lives large in higher education that asking for help is a sign of indecision or weakness and that somehow, they should know everything they need to know about their role's responsibilities, challenges, and complexities. As explained in *Smart People Ask for (My) Advice: Seeking Advice Boosts Perceptions of Competence* asking for help, support, and advice before it is too late is almost always a smart and courageous thing to do. One of higher education's greatest assets are the willingness of people to provide support and assistance, *if asked.* The "collegial" nature of many of our campuses encourages helping others. While it's true that on some toxic campuses, asking for help would not be the smart thing to do as it's seen as a sign of incompetence and weakness—such campuses are the exception, not the rule.

Institutional Strategies for Preventing Derailment

1. Senior Leaders Need to Discuss the Issue of Derailment With All Their Direct Reports

Identify an article or book to discuss at a yearly *"chew and chat"* (such as a working breakfast or lunch) where small groups talk about the implications of derailment and how to prevent it from happening on their campus. Senior leadership has to model the way and participate, and fully support these yearly (at least) discussions. Their authentic involvement will communicate that it is an important issue for the campus to consider and that leaders have specific expectations for the behaviors that will and will not be tolerated on their campus.

2. Design and Institutionalize Effective Supervisory Processes

Effective supervision is one of the most effective ways to avoid derailment as it provides the necessary ongoing feedback for all employees and helps ensure that inappropriate behavior is stopped in its tracks. It should build on the strengths of the employee but also be direct and honest about areas of needed development. An annual supervisory exercise is inadequate. Effective supervision takes real time and attention for leaders to do it well, and the investment almost always pays off with motivated employees, better performance, and fewer derailing behaviors. Effective supervision can constructively interfere with the derailing process, because it provides timely feedback, advice, and perspective.

For an example of an effective supervisory dialogue, see the Appendix at the end of this book.

3. Simply Do Not Tolerate Volatile and Inappropriate Behavior

There is never, ever, a good reason for a leader to berate an employee.

CASE STUDY

During a meeting, the vice president for enrollment began to unravel because he wasn't hitting his enrollment targets and started berating marketing and retention efforts by his colleagues. The president quietly and quickly intervened by calling a recess. She spoke with the vice president for enrollment in private and clearly stated her expectations for appropriate behavior, respectfully and directly asking if he thought he could discuss the issue appropriately. The VP agreed and the meeting continued. The president maintained the dignity of the vice president and clearly communicated her expectations for appropriate behavior in her meetings.

---

4. Deep Mentoring

"Those who have torches will pass them onto others." - Plato

As young people begin to migrate up their career ladder, they need access to wise and trusted advice. Every senior leader on a campus should model the way by mentoring emerging leaders several layers down in the organization. This communicates to all campus stakeholders that the institution is committed to developing its leaders. These mentors can provide strategic insight, counsel, and support for leaders who are learning *how* to lead. Mentoring must be supported in the performance review process by recognizing and rewarding those leaders who help grow others. Unless the supervisory process includes a leader's ability to mentor others, it may not become an institutional priority or practice. Many senior leaders are already overwhelmed within their day-to-day responsibilities. Finding time to mentor and motivate someone can be a major effort, and institutional support is essential.

Avoid "Comfortable Cloning"

"Comfortable cloning" is the tendency to hire and develop potential and emerging leaders who are *similar* to us (e.g., background, gender, race, leadership style, and education), because we are "comfortable" with them. This subconscious cloning process could have a powerful and adverse influence on *who* we mentor and develop. I would suggest that mentors *"cross a boundary"* when selecting emerging leaders to help grow and develop. If they can select someone from a different race, gender, or life experience, the leadership leverage that is achieved can be powerful.

Be Conscious of "Stylistic Invisibles"

Linda Hill from Harvard provides us with this intriguing and provocative term. She is describing an embedded bias many of us have. There are certain people who don't "fit" our conventional image of what a leader "should" look like. They tend to be quiet, reserved, and highly competent contributors who act with integrity and care. They do not seek the limelight, recognition, or praise but possess many leadership qualities. They need to be identified and mentored effectively. The high potentials and "charismatic" emerging leaders are easy to identify, while the "invisibles" are harder to detect, but worth the extra effort.

5. Provide Developmental Assignments

This is where effective, disciplined and supportive supervision comes into the picture. Every supervisor should understand the strengths and weaknesses of all their direct reports. This enables them to select appropriate developmental assignments that will build on the strengths and develop the weaknesses of their people. There needs to be a balanced approach to the allocation of these learning experiences so that the assignments aren't all "stretch" assignments focused on their areas of weakness. Careful and thoughtful selection of these relevant tasks can build the leadership muscles of their direct reports. The supervisor's direct reports need to understand the rationale behind the assignments, how it will contribute to their learning and development, and how it adds value to campus efforts to move forward.

For example:

1. An emerging leader might be asked to serve on a campus wide strategic planning task force. Which

will enable them to work with colleagues across the campus and to meet some of the real players and scholars within the institution. They will learn about strategic thinking, environmental analysis, collaborative problem solving, and institutional values. Most importantly, they will begin to develop the *relational capital* they will need to conduct cross-boundary work in service of the institution's vision and goals.

2. They can serve on local community development committees and task forces, which will expose them to external stakeholders' perspectives and provide them with a picture of how the campus is seen by "outsiders" in the surrounding community. Often they learn about the real challenges too many of our communities face, like poverty, obtaining a quality education, food scarcity, or violent neighborhoods.

3. They can head a task force to improve campus-wide or divisional communications. This will help them build their influence skills, especially if those participating on the task force don't report to them. Organizing a coherent and agile communication process takes a systems perspective and can teach the leader "how" things actually work on their campus. The combination of the nuts and bolts details of effective communication and more sophisticated processes (like ensuring quality control, managing the rumor mill, creating diverse communication vehicles, and developing feedback mechanisms) can be a game changer for an emerging leader.

The purpose of these developmental assignments is to help build their leadership portfolio both wide (across campus boundaries) and deep (develop a content expertise). Their supervisors need to meet with them periodically throughout the learning journey, not just at the end of the assignment, to identify what they are learning, what insights they are gaining, difficulties they are encountering, and what support they need.

For many years, researchers at The Center For Creative Leadership have found that "embedded work," which is the real work leaders do every day, is one of the most powerful and effective ways to develop leadership.

6. Watch Out for "Fast Tracking" a Young and Emerging Leader

It's easy to be impressed with a sharp, quick-on-their-feet, charismatic "doer." Hopes and aspirations loom large and can hide their many limitations. Make sure they develop a well-rounded portfolio of skills and qualities before promoting them, rewarding them with high profile assignments, or sending them to prestigious courses and programs. Moving them through the ranks too quickly can accelerate the derailing process.

Avoid testing high potentials by giving them complex and difficult assignments and letting them "fend" for themselves. This is the old "baptism by fire" approach that lived large in many organizations for decades. Challenges are part of the learning process for sure, but they need to be supported by good supervision, ongoing feedback, and effective coaching—and not just with the mentality that "what doesn't kill you makes you stronger."

7. Remember the "Stylistic Invisibles"

These individuals often possess huge leadership potential but, somehow, are "invisible" to us because they don't fit our *mental model* of what leaders look like. They don't seek attention or praise; instead, they produce results, act with integrity, and treat people with care. All of these are essential leadership qualities.

Interested leaders are encouraged to read *Leading Quietly: An Unorthodox Guide to Doing the Right Thing* (2002) by Joseph Badaracco, who describes such individuals as possessing the virtues of restraint, modesty, and tenacity. We need more of these kinds of leaders on our campuses.

Senior leaders need to "grow" a diverse set of leaders throughout our campuses, and we must be diligent about *how* we select emerging leaders to develop. Pay attention to the introverts and quiet ones; the charismatic ones are always easy to identify.

8. Manage Leadership Transitions Carefully

When a leader moves up the career ladder or to another division or school on campus, it can be a fragile time. There will be different cultural norms, expectations, and rules. Very rarely are these ever written down somewhere, and the new leader has to figure things out. Some tried and true behaviors will be acceptable; some will not. What worked in the previous job may not work anymore.

The supervisor of a transitioning leader needs to pay close attention to the process, especially if the leader is new to the campus. The Society for Human Resource Management (SHRM) has identified a model/framework called the 4C's, which they use for onboarding new employees:

    A. **COMPLIANCE:** This is the nuts and bolts, where new employees are taught the legal and policy regulations of the organization by HR or a supervisor.

B. CLARIFICATION: Making sure that the new employee understands their new job and related expectations is an important part of the supervisor's responsibility. These different expectations need to be communicated carefully over time; it is not enough to cram a lot of information into one meeting and then ask if there are any questions. Instead, it should be several conversations where the supervisor probes for understanding, gives the new employee time to develop questions, and makes sure that everyone is on the same page.

C. CULTURE: This is the most critical part of the transition process, where the supervisor provides the transitioning leader with a sense of organizational norms, both formal and informal. This must be done thoughtfully and patiently. It is essential that the new leader understand the complexity, nuance, and mystery of the new place's culture to avoid a "cultural mismatch" where the new person starts to derail early because they are left to bump into tradition, people, hidden beliefs, and "the way we do things around here." Explain in explicit terms, what is accepted, what works, and what isn't tolerated. Do not let them figure it out for themselves; that's a recipe for disaster. It is also helpful to have several colleagues share what they think are the cultural norms and tell some stories that reflect the culture of the new organization.

D. CONNECTION: The supervisor needs to help the transitioning leader develop the interpersonal relationships they will need in others to work with others successfully. The supervisor needs to arrange specific meetings and opportunities to get to know key employees. These are opportunities to build a relational connection with others and must be carefully crafted to ensure maximum benefit. Beginnings are important; take the time to do it right.

The second "Connection" element is identifying the information network the transitioning leader will need to be successful. Identify who they need to talk with to get information, perspective, advice, and answers to questions. The supervisor needs to make the introductions for these individuals and help the new leader build their own information network as fast as possible.

9. Watch Out for Workload

It is important that leaders and supervisors monitor the workload of all their direct reports. It's common on campuses to find too much work piled onto too-full plates, which dedicated and hard working people find difficult to turn down. Because so many people are dedicated to the missions of their institutions, they put in extra effort and time to accomplish the goals and objectives of their campus. However, when followers don't want to disappoint their boss, or don't see them working as hard, they often take on more work than they can do or should do. Quality over time begins to decline, and people grow frustrated because they know that their work standards are lower than they want them to be. It is a vicious trap and supervisors are usually the culprits here. They need to be acutely aware of this dynamic and help their direct reports manage both their expectations and their workload. The key thing to remember here is that too much work can trigger the derailment process.

10. Consider Senior Leadership Dialogues, Not Monologues

No institution needs a series of "talking heads" sharing their wit and wisdom about leadership with aspiring and emerging leaders. Senior leaders need to share their successes *and* their failures so emerging leaders understand that nobody reaches the senior levels of leadership without making mistakes. Such conversations change the climate of the room and encourage an authentic conversation about real leadership. It is a gift that too few senior leaders have the courage to share. Consider sharing:

- What guiding principles helped you lead through a difficult situation?

- How do you develop the toughness to make hard decisions—and yet remain sensitive to the needs of others?

- How do you build trust on a campus? What have you done to rebuild trust once it has been damaged?

- Who do you talk with during difficult times? Do you have supporters and confidants?

- Do you feel guilty about some of the decisions you have made?

- Who are your leadership heroes? Who do you admire and respect? Why?

- As a leader have you ever felt lost or confused? How did you respond?

- When you look back on your leadership journey, what are two important lessons you would be willing to share?

- How do you take care of yourself? How do you seek balance in your life?

- What was an ethical dilemma you witnessed or faced? What did you do?

- What are some of your strengths that you have to be conscious of not overdoing?

These simple yet powerful questions can create a rare conversation that is a memorable learning experience for emerging leaders. It separates all the theory and platitudes about leadership and discusses leadership honestly, warts and all. This kind of dialogue is essential to helping aspiring leaders realize that:

- It is smart to ask for help when you are in trouble.

- Honesty and integrity are the lifeblood of authentic leadership, and without them, you can not lead.

- There is a difference between "smartship" and leadership.

- Making mistakes is inevitable and part of the leadership journey.

- Leading a team is a privilege.

- Aspiration is nobler than ambition and appetite.

- Trust is a "strategic asset" that every leader needs in order to lead others.

11. Consider Giving Derailing Leaders a Sabbatical

This notion might sound somewhat counterintuitive, but can work:

Example A

One example is of a dean of a large college. He was ambitious, a brilliant academic, and wanted someday to become a president, but he was experiencing some difficulty in his new role. In his first term, he encountered many challenges, mostly interpersonal and relational in nature, and was unable to understand why his faculty colleagues couldn't see how smart his ideas were. He began to crumble toward the end of the first semester, and it became obvious that he might fail in his first deanship. The president intervened and suggested that he take a one semester sabbatical on two conditions: first, the dean had to go through a 360° feedback process and gather anonymous data on how he was seen by his colleagues. Second, he had to agree to an executive coach who would review the data with him. He readily agreed to both.

He returned after a semester with a game plan to deal with his shortcomings. He met with his department chairs to share in broad strokes what he had learned. He encouraged them to be open and honest with him in the future, and if they thought he wasn't listening, flag the issue. This took courage, and he gained the respect and support of his people. He has been a successful dean for several years and is considering being a president soon.

Example B

In another case, a vice president of student affairs was going through a difficult set of personal setbacks (i.e. his father was ill, and he was in the middle of a divorce). This leader was well liked and respected, but started to blow up at meetings. He became critical of his direct reports in public and was under-performing his assigned responsibilities.

The vice president of human resources met with the president to relay her concerns about the situation and together they met with the vice president of student affairs. He was given a month off to take care of his family and personal needs. This created the breathing space he needed to collect his thoughts and feelings and come up with a plan to deal with the two challenging situations.

He returned in a month and committed to the president that he would not exhibit the inappropriate behaviors again. He kept his word, and began to do a good job once again.

There are no guarantees with these kinds of sabbaticals, and some campuses might not be able to provide this kind of practice for their derailing leaders. But if possible, it's important to consider all creative approaches.

Summary

Derailment lives large in higher education, but remains hidden. This is understandable, as sensitive issues are always difficult to talk about; it can be embarrassing for both the individual and the institution. However, in a society where 50% of leaders and managers fail, institutions should be proactive and openly discuss this issue on campuses to avoid losing so many promising leaders. Leadership is essential to success in higher education, and derailment takes away from the overall ability of an institution to move ahead.

Not a hot topic, but an important one.

References

Anderson, Merrill C., et al. *Creating Coaching Cultures: What Business Leaders Expect and Strategies to Get There.* White Paper, Center for Creative Leadership, 2009.

Ashkenas, Ron, et al. "Rebounding from Career Setbacks." *Harvard Business Review,* October 2014.

Brooks, A.W., et al. "Smart People Ask for (My) Advice: Seeking Advice Boosts Perceptions of Competence." *Management Science,* vol. 61, no. 6 June 2015, pp. 1421–1435.

Canfield, Jack, and Peter Chee. *Coaching for Breakthrough Success: Proven Techniques for Making Impossible Dreams Possible.* McGraw-Hill, 2013.

Capretta, Cara, et al. "Executive Derailment: Three Cases in Point and How to Prevent It." *Global Business and Organizational Excellence,* vol. 27, no. 3, March/April 2008, pp. 48-56.

Charan, Ram. "Ending the CEO Succession Crisis." *Harvard Business Review,* February 2005.

Dotlich, David L., and Peter C. Cairo. *Why CEOs Fail: The 11 Behaviors That Can Derail Your Climb to the Top--and How to Manage Them.* Jossey-Bass, 2003.

Dotlich, David and James L. Noel. *Action Learning: How the World's Top Companies are Re-Creating their Leaders and Themselves.* Jossey-Bass, 1998.

Fernandez-Araoz, Claudio, et al. "How to Hang on to Your High Potentials." *Harvard Business Review,* October 2011.

Fisher, Anne. "Starting a New Job? Don't Blow It." *Fortune*, 7 March 2005.

Furnham, Adrian, and John Taylor. *The Elephant in the Boardroom: The Causes of Leadership Derailment*. Palgrave Macmillan, 2010.

Gentry, William A. "Derailment: How Successful Leaders Avoid It." *Association for Talent Development*, 25 January 2011.

Gentry, William A. and L. R. Shanock. "Views of Managerial Derailment from Above & Below: The Importance of a Good Relationship with Upper Management and Putting People at Ease." *Journal of Applied Psychology*, no. 38: 2469-2494, 2008.

Goldsmith, Marshall, and Mark Reiter. *What Got You Here Won't Get You There: How Successful People Become Even More Successful*. Hyperion, 2007.

Goleman, Daniel. *Emotional Intelligence: Why It Can Matter More Than IQ*. Bantam Books, 2005.

—. *Working with Emotional Intelligence*. Bantam Books, 2000.

Goleman, Daniel, et al. *Primal Leadership: Realizing the Power of Emotional Intelligence*. Harvard Business Review Press, 2002.

—. *Primal Leadership: Unleashing the Power of Emotional Intelligence*. Harvard Business Review Press, 2013.

Goldsmith, Marshall, with Mark Reiter. *What Got You Here Won't Get You There: How Successful People Become Even More Successful!* Hyperion, 2007.

Heifetz, Ronald A., and Martin Linsky. *Leadership on the Line: Staying Alive Through the Dangers of Leading.* Harvard Business School Press, 2002.

Hernez-Broome, Gina, and Richard L. Hughes. "Leadership Development: Past, Present, and Future." *Human Resource Planning,* 2004, pp. 24-32.

Hogan, Joyce, et al. "Management Derailment." *American Psychological Handbook of Industrial and Organizational Psychology,* vol. 3, American Psychological Association, pp. 555-575.

Hughes, Richard, et al. *Leadership: Enhancing the Lessons of Experience.* McGraw-Hill/Irwin, 2011.

Inyang, Benjamin James. "Exploring the Concept of Leadership Derailment: Defining New Research Agenda." *International Journal of Business and Management,* vol. 8, no. 16, 2013, pp. 78-85.

Irwin, Tim. *Derailed: Five Lessons Learned from Catastrophic Failures of Leadership.* Thomas Nelson, 2012.

Kaiser, Robert B. *The Perils of Accentuating the Positive.* Hogan Press, 2009.

Kaplan, Robert E., and Robert B. Kaiser. *Fear Your Strengths: What You Are Best at Could Be Your Biggest Problem.* Berrett-Koehler Publishers, 2103.

Linsky, Martin, and Ronald A. Heifetz. *Leadership on the Line: Staying Alive through the Dangers of Leading.* Harvard Business School Publishing, 2002.

Lombardo, Michael M., and Robert W. Eichinger. *Preventing Derailment: What to Do Before It's Too Late.* Center for Creative Leadership, 1989.

—. *The Leadership Machine: Architecture to Develop Leaders for Any Future.* Lominger Ltd Inc., 2000.

Marks, Mitchell Lee, et al. "Rebounding from Career Setbacks." *Harvard Business Review*, October 2014.

McCall, Morgan W., and Michael M. Lombardo. *Off the Track: Why and How Successful Executives Get Derailed.* Center for Creative Leadership, 1983.

McCauley, Cynthia D., et al. *Experience- Driven Leader Development: Models, Tools, Best Practices and Advice for On-the- Job Development.* John Wiley, 2010.

McCauley, Cynthia and Michael M. Lombardo. "Benchmarks: An Instrument for Diagnosing Managerial Strengths and Weaknesses." *Measures of Leadership.* K. E. Clark and M. B. Clark, eds. Center for Creative Leadership, 1990, pp. 535-545.

Moxley, R. S. and Wilson O'Connor. "A Systems Approach to Leadership Development." *The Center for Creative Leadership Handbook of Leadership Development.* C. D. McCauley, R. S. Moxley, and E. Van Velsor, eds. Jossey-Bass, 1998.

Ready, Douglas A. "Is Your Company Failing Its Leaders?" *Business Strategy Review*, vol. 16, no. 4, 2005, pp. 21-25.

Sanaghan, Patrick. *5 Secrets to Developing a High-Performing Team in Higher Education.* Academic Impressions, 2014.

Sanaghan, Patrick, and Kimberly Eberbach. *Creating the Exceptional Team: A Practitioner's Guide.* H R D Press, 2014.

Sanaghan, Patrick, et al. *Presidential Transitions: It's Not Just the Position, It's the Transition*. Rowman & Littlefield Education, 2009.

Sanaghan, Patrick, and Susan Jurow. "Who Will Step into Your Shoes?" *Business Officer*, vol. 44, no. 10, 2011, pp. 16-24.

Trotta, Melissa K. "Growing Our Own: The Institutional and Individual Value of an On-Campus Leadership Development Program for Higher Educational Administrators." Doctoral dissertation, University of Pennsylvania, 2014.

Weinstock, Beth, and Mary Ellen Smith Glasgow. "Executive Coaching to Support Doctoral Role Transitions and Promote Leadership Consciousness." *Role Development for Doctoral Advanced Nursing Practice*, Springer Publishing Company, 2010.

Weinstock, Beth. "The Benefits of a Leadership Program and Executive Coaching for New Nursing Administrators: One College's Experience." *Journal of Professional Nursing*, 2009.

Weinzimmer, Lawrence G., and Jim McConnoughy. *The Wisdom of Failure: How to Learn the Tough Leadership Lessons without Paying the Price*. Jossey-Bass, 2012.

Wood Brooks, Alison, et al. *Smart People Ask for (My) Advice: Seeking Advice Boosts Perceptions of Competence*. Harvard Business School Working Papers, 2014.

Zaccaro, Stephen J. *The Nature of Executive Leadership: A Conceptual and Empirical Analysis of Success*. American Psychological Association, 2001.

Zenger, John, and Joseph Folkman. "Ten fatal flaws that derail leaders." *Harvard Business Review*, 2009.

——. *The Extraordinary Leader: Turning Good Managers into Great Leaders.* McGraw Hill, 2009.

CHAPTER 2
THE SEDUCTION OF THE LEADER: A DYNAMIC TO AVOID

Overview

How often have you thought: "My people always tell me what's *really* going on." Hundreds of leaders have told us that their followers are open with them. These leaders believed that they were getting honest feedback and were being asked the tough questions. Unfortunately, this is rarely true. In fact, we've come to think of this common belief as a myth—a myth consistent with the concept of *seduction of the leader*, which was introduced to us more than twenty-five years ago by our colleague Dr. Rod Napier.

Many leaders in higher education are seduced by the notion that they're receiving honest and thoughtful feedback about their ideas and effectiveness. Believing this leaves leaders isolated and uninformed.

Why are leaders not receiving honest information? Because most followers avoid "speaking truth to power." They avoid it for a variety of reasons, reasons we'll explore shortly. But whatever the reasons, the unfortunate consequence of this reluctance to speak frankly is that you, the leader, lack access to the vital information you need to make effective decisions, grow, and learn—*even when you have asked for it.*

Based upon our years of observation and work with leaders in higher education, corporations, and nonprofit institutions, we understand *seduction of the leader* as a pervasive syndrome that is always present in the lives of leaders. This is worth repeating, it is *always* present and that is why, as we will explain, it is so pernicious. Before you can employ strategies to counter this dynamic, you'll need to become aware of its existence and of its powerful implications for your leadership.

What Does *Seduction of the Leader* Look Like?

As we've asserted, leaders are always at risk of being seduced into believing they're on the right path and avoiding evidence to the contrary. The following three types of seduction—seduction by sycophants, seduction by great expectations, and seduction by ego—are the types we've seen most often.

Seduction by Sycophants

Several years ago, we met with a new university president and his informal "kitchen cabinet." Although there was an official senior team in place as well, these three individuals helped the president develop ideas, shape policy, and make decisions. We'd been invited to explore with the president and his three top advisors how the university could implement a strategic plan. Since we'd been referred to the new president by his trusted mentor, who had worked with us previously, we believed that the table had been set nicely for us, so to speak, and we were eager to share our expertise.

During our two meetings with the president and his kitchen cabinet, however, we experienced the detrimental effects of seduction by sycophants. Although this new leader had never conducted a strategic-planning process, this didn't stop him from strongly stating his misinformed ideas. Nor did it stop his cabinet from readily praising and agreeing with everything he said. When we provided counter-advice or a different perspective, our contribution was quickly shot down by the cabinet. This was rather peculiar, given that we've designed and led over a hundred strategic-planning projects and have gained much expertise as a result. We've even written books on the subject.

The first meeting was particularly difficult. By the second meeting, we knew what to expect. We were more assertive with our advice, hoping to get it past the kitchen cabinet; we wanted the president to have as much accurate information as possible so that he could make informed decisions. Yet, when we shared our differing opinions and perspectives, the cabinet members dismissed them. They acted as if we didn't know what we were talking about. They attacked our rationales, questioned our understanding of the complexities of their organization, and were surprisingly rude.

Once again, they accepted whatever the president stated as the truth, bestowed it with glowing compliments, and ignored our contributions. The cabinet members were clearly intelligent and thoughtful people, but they were not serving their leader well that day. He may have been surrounded by people he trusted, but he was alone with his uninformed positions.

If you aren't getting feedback that is challenging, being asked tough questions, or hearing contrary opinions, you can bet that seduction by sycophants is alive and well. We'll share some proactive and practical advice on how to avoid this particular seduction dynamic later in this chapter.

Seduction by Great Expectations

We encountered a different sort of seduction of the leader when asked to advise an experienced university president with a track record of success. She inherited an institution that had been going downhill slowly for years. As its faculty members were aging, they were becoming less productive; student enrollment was declining; the institutional brand was vague and confusing; and the endowment was anemic.

This institution desperately needed vitality, clarity, and focus. Tough decisions were needed to turn this ship around. The board believed the new president was right for the job because she had vision, energy, and great ideas. She was known for being a decisive and compassionate leader who got things done.

Unfortunately, when she arrived, many campus stakeholders had a long list of demands and expectations for the new president. They wanted her to cure the pervasive complacency, rebuild the academic reputation and productivity of the faculty, create a powerful and clear brand, increase enrollment, and oh, by the way, raise fifty million dollars for the endowment.

This president was captured by the unrealistic expectations of her followers and became convinced that she could pull them all off by herself. She began to put in seventy-hour weeks. Her schedule was too full, and she was trying to do too much. But who was going to tell this respected, hardworking, and engaging leader to slow down? Things were beginning to move forward. Campus enthusiasm was palatable. Students just loved the new president, and donors were beginning to be generous again.

The board chair was smart enough to know that the president could not keep up this overwhelming pace. He communicated his concerns privately to the president on several occasions, asking her to slow down. Unfortunately, he was the only one telling her this, and his advice fell on deaf ears.

We were brought in to do a first-year assessment of the new president. After conducting interviews with faculty, staff, and senior team members, we determined several important things: the president needed to create a shared sense of ownership and responsibility going forward, she needed to manage the expectations of multiple stakeholders in order to make them more realistic, and—as her board ally had told her repeatedly—she needed to slow down. We also learned that many people were concerned about the president's health but were unwilling to say anything. They were afraid that if she slowed down, all of the things she was holding together would quickly unravel.

We delivered the news. The president thanked us warmly for our guidance, then ignored it completely. She had a mild heart attack several months later, which might have been avoided if more people had insisted that she needed to reduce her workload or, better yet, had helped her with it. But this fact is key: The president was given vital information by several key people that she chose to ignore. She decided instead that she alone could pull this campus out of its rut. Dazzled by the high expectations of her stakeholders and the illusion that she could meet them all, she didn't listen to sound advice to the contrary. She was willing to be seduced by the adulation and appreciation of others.

If you find yourself working way too hard and too long and feeling exhausted, it's time to ask yourself some tough questions, starting with these:

- Why am I working so hard? What drives me to do all this hard work?

- Can I ask for help? Who can help me?

- What are the effects of my overwork on my family and on me?

- What do I need to change now?

Leaders often find being at the center of things very attractive. Being really important to everyone, serving as a hero, and being the only one who can pull things off can be very seductive. But you're not the only one who can pull things off. There are usually plenty of people around to help, but you must enlist their support, ask for help, and pace yourself to sustain your stamina. There is no study in the world that shows that working seventy-plus hours a week is productive and effective.

Seduction by Ego

A brilliant scientist became president of a research institute. He was well known in his field for his scientific accomplishments and had earned two PhDs. It was commonly acknowledged in his professional arena that he was very smart and talented. But he felt a need to assert his brilliance to an extent that worked against him. He sucked the air out of any room he entered by moving to the center of conversations and acting as if he was the only person with ideas. He came across as arrogant and self-centered. People didn't like him much.

The negative impact of this person's leadership on the institute emerged quickly. People became uninterested in what he had to say. They never asked questions in their meetings with him (almost always a bad sign), and they texted back and forth about what a blowhard he was. Attendance at the monthly research meetings was dwindling and grant funders began to stop taking his phone calls.

How does one tell this brilliant but arrogant leader that he needs to change his leadership style dramatically if he doesn't want to fail? And who will deliver this message?

Fortunately, leadership audits were a common tradition within the institution, one started by a wise provost several years before. We were called in as we had been every two years or so to conduct an audit. To our surprise, the brilliant scientist learned something.

We will discuss leadership audits in more detail later. In essence, we gathered anonymous data via multiple conversations with individuals in the scientist's sphere of influence. We learned a lot. He was respected but not at all liked. In fact, some of his peers were waiting—even hoping—for him to fail. We were able to translate what we learned into three strong recommendations.

We braced ourselves for the conversation, expecting him to refuse to deal with his impact on others. But we were delighted to be surprised. Not only did our brilliant scientist listen; he also acknowledged that he had received this kind of feedback previously and that his wife regularly poked fun at the size of his ego. Our client's ego did not shrink as a result of this feedback, but he was able to put a plan in place that allowed him to identify nonverbal cues that signaled he was bulldozing others. He became able to recognize those cues—and to stop the bulldozing.

To get a sense of whether you are vulnerable to seduction by ego, consider the following questions:

- Am I aware of my impact on people in our meetings and conversations? If so, how do I see myself influencing their behavior? If not, how can I become more aware of my impact and how it affects others' behavior?

- Do I need to be center stage all the time? If so, how can I be more aware and actively invite others into the limelight?

- Do I share credit with others? If not, what mechanisms can I put in place that will trigger kudos for those around me?

- Am I a good listener? If not, how can I put signals in place to remind me to be more curious and appreciative of others' experience and point of view?

- Do I ask others for their advice and perspectives? If not, who can I call upon starting tomorrow to change this pattern?

How Does *Seduction of the Leader* Occur?

In virtually every organization we've observed over the years, those with less power and influence often have great difficulty communicating anything but positive or benign information to those with more power and influence. People lack the skill, courage, or both to ask tough questions, share difficult information, or offer contrary points of view to their leaders.

As a result, most of the senior leaders we have witnessed, including university presidents, chief executive officers, executive vice presidents, and board chairs, are not finding out about important matters such as these:

Competing agendas. When the leader is unaware of the interests of an important stakeholder group that conflicts with their priorities and direction, there's trouble ahead. For example, a sales team might be in love with a traditional product that is easy to sell and might not be as enthused about a new product that will take a lot of effort to launch and that will change the compensation model. This will affect the new product's chances of success.

Significant gaps in organizational capabilities. When an institution lacks the talent, expertise, or resources to do what it has committed to doing, people may know that they lack the bandwidth to take on a new challenge, but they won't say anything. They may go along to get along, hoping for the best and producing predictably mediocre results.

Impending market changes. When there are financial, technological, or environmental forces on the horizon that will take the organization by surprise, some people in the organization may anticipate these dramatic changes and understand their implications. But that information may never make it to the right people, because those who are looking ahead lack access to key decision makers and strategists.

Failing projects with unachievable goals. When a project is in the red and beyond saving, who will warn the leader about this upcoming failure? A great deal of money may have already been invested, and there's no Plan B. Some people saw the problems emerging a long time ago, but no one said anything. Now the project has become a money pit.

Blind spots or unwarranted loyalties. When a leader is enamored with someone, the leader may have unrealistic expectations of that person's abilities. Everyone may know the person just doesn't have the talent, but they won't share this knowledge with the leader. The "golden" child fails, and people murmur, "I told you so."

The impact of behavior on key constituents. When a leader's own behavior blocks information from coming through, the leader needs to be told. For example, a leader's creative and entrepreneurial spirit might be undermining an institution's ability to get necessary blocking and tackling done. If that leader tells others, "Don't bother me with the details," people will become reluctant to point out that the "details" are preventing the leader from being successful.

Serious incompetence on the senior team. When there are people on the leader's team who don't have the requisite expertise to pull their own weight, the leader needs to know. Perhaps team members are nice— incompetent, but nice. People may be reluctant to alert the leader, both because this would hurt people's feelings and because it might injure the group's collegial climate.

Although our examples of the impacts of seduction are at the senior level, *anyone* in a leadership position—a manager, a director, an associate vice president, and so on—can fall victim to the seduction dynamic. *Anyone.* The seduction of the leader is always present and always has the potential to be destructive.

Sometimes, it's not your behavior but the intentions of others that confound your efforts. More often than our ideals would like us to admit, we have seen leaders being intentionally undermined. But the *seduction of the leader* dynamic is not fueled by malice. Individuals who fail to bring critical information to you are often loyal and dedicated. While the outcome may be the same, their reluctance isn't driven by a desire to deceive, misinform, or undermine your effectiveness or ultimate success.

We have worked with leaders who've had the discipline and courage to build teams and cultures in which respectful disagreement and "rough and tumble" dialogue were encouraged and rewarded. But they are the exception. What happens much more frequently is that leaders receive only watered-down versions of the truth, versions designed to lighten the negative impact of necessary information.

In a campus environment, for example, we've witnessed crucial information being weakened with phrases like "faculty always complain" or "I can assure you that other campuses have more serious problems than this." Although there may be truth in these statements, they mask important messages in order to make them more palatable for the leader.

Several years ago, we attended a meeting at which the mayor of a large city made a speech about his vision for the future to a hundred or so senior-level administrators. The mayor was excited about the possibilities he saw for his city, and he spoke with passion and enthusiasm. After an hour or so, he was finally done. Almost as an afterthought, as he was heading out of the room, he asked attendees if they had any questions. He was met with silence.

He then left, believing that he had hit a home run. Unfortunately, he didn't hear the dissent that ensued when he left the room. People mumbled to each other, sharing doubts and reservations, wondering how they were ever going to accomplish even half of what his vision entailed. They milled around for over an hour, grumbling, complaining, and discussing their reactions to and reservations about the mayor's "vision."

Unfortunately, the mayor never heard their thoughts. He believed that his people got it and were ready to move forward. They didn't, and they weren't. He was clueless about how his people really felt. How successful do you think he has been in implementing his vision?

This scenario happens throughout many organizations every day. We have witnessed it countless times ourselves. The setting doesn't have to be an important speech; it can play out in small meetings and forums, too, in which line managers, superintendents, and directors share their ideas, weakly ask for reactions, and rarely get anything meaningful in return.

If the mayor really wanted input and feedback, he could have utilized a simple device to encourage conversation. This is a device that you can use with your people. It will have a powerful impact, *if* you want a real conversation. You can say some version of the following: "I know I've covered a lot of territory here and shared a lot of big ideas. I really want your questions and reactions. Please turn to the person next to you and have a conversation for a couple of minutes about your responses. Please come up with one question together that you'd like to ask." After people have the chance to talk, you can then say, "Please share your thinking with me."

A word of caution here. Be sure you have left at least 30 minutes for questions. It will not be productive for you to cut these off. If you believe time will be limited, hand out index cards and ask each pair to write their question down. This will allow you to take questions for 30 minutes *and* not lose valuable data. If you go this route, you must create an opportunity to reply to the unanswered questions within a reasonable period of time, say one week. This response could take place at another face-to-face meeting or through a written reply.

This device sounds simple, but it is powerful, and it will almost always create a rich conversation. People *always* have reactions to what is being said. Your task is to find out how to get them to have a real conversation, so you can benefit from their input.

What Are the Underlying Dynamics of *Seduction of the Leader*?

For years we've been investigating the origins of the seduction dilemma. By figuring out the underlying dynamics, we can support leaders better by giving them signs to look out for and intentional strategies to use to counter its influence. We've identified four primary dynamics that are usually in play: 1) the leader's response to information, 2) the leader's response to honest feedback, 3) the weight of tradition, and 4) gatekeepers.

Dynamic 1: The Leader's Response to Information

First and foremost, as a leader, your own response to information can invoke reticence in others. If people experience a negative reaction (e.g., anger, denying, or arguing) when they deliver unpleasant or contrary news to you, you can bet that they'll be reluctant to share such news with you in the future. And there will be a ripple effect; how you react to negative or contrary news and perspectives will become well known among your people. If you have a reputation for being reactive, you will be seduced by sycophants instead of receiving honest information or feedback.

Fixing this may sound simple, but it isn't. People are always watching your reactions and responses *very* carefully. When you hold a leadership role, think of your behavior as being magnified. You need to be very aware of how you react to unpleasant news and information and to practice responding in a welcoming way, because even a subtle negative reaction can send a potent message to your people that will be hard to change.

Dynamic 2: The Leader's Response to Honest Feedback

People's desire to be included, to have influence, and to keep their seat at the table can be powerful reasons not to tell it like it is. If people perceive that being honest can be a career-limiting move, you can bet that truth will not be told. When forthright folks are disinvited to important meetings or conversations or find themselves out of the information loop, the message is clear: bad news is a professional liability. This news *will* move like quicksilver throughout the organization, and its damage will be very difficult to undo.

It's easier to start out on the right footing than to undo such damage. The effort you'll have to expend to demonstrate that it's okay to speak up after an episode showing the contrary will be enormous, and not everyone will believe you. Even just one or two examples of the negative consequences of speaking up will become a permanent part of the organization's legend and lore.

We witnessed a situation in which a new school superintendent had several meetings with his school principals over the summer to plan for the upcoming year. Several times during the three days of meetings, a well-respected, experienced, and assertive elementary school principal pushed back on some of the ideas that the new superintendent proposed and asked him some tough questions. This behavior was not well received.

Soon afterward, the superintendent transferred the outspoken principal to the toughest high school in the city under the guise that he was putting his best people in the most challenging situations. The powerful message this conveyed to all the principals and administrators in the district was that those who spoke truth to power would be punished severely. The superintendent's punitive behavior sent shock waves throughout the district.

Because of this, the superintendent never received contrary or honest information or feedback about his leadership effectiveness and actions. He was gone in less than two years, leaving behind a mess—a bucketful of mistrust and a group of principals who were very worried about what the next superintendent would be like.

Dynamic 3: The Weight of Tradition

An institution's history and traditions can create barriers instead of acting as bridges to openness, feedback, and honest exchange. To make matters worse, followers typically perceive an executive leader as representing the institution itself, with all its power, politics, and history. This perception can make them reluctant to push back on the leader's ideas for fear of seeming disrespectful to the leader's role or to the institution. This occurs commonly at large institutions, including universities, hospitals, and sizeable nonprofits.

While a strong sense of community often exists in such settings, this collegial atmosphere doesn't make truth-telling easy. As a leader, you need to consider the potential impact of your organization's traditions, values, and history on your people. They may find the weight and authority of the institution so heavy that speaking honestly may seem unwise, even impossible.

So what can you do? In your work, you can model not only respect for the institution but also flexibility and openness. This can send the message that it's okay to change. You can also speak about the strengths of your organization's history and traditions and about the importance of not allowing these to inhibit growth and the possibilities the future holds.

Dynamic 4: Gatekeepers

Those with authority are often shielded from critical information because well-meaning gatekeepers block access, intending to protect their leaders' time. These gatekeepers believe that it is their role, even their duty, to keep the onslaught of information and demands at bay.

One of our colleagues had a loyal executive assistant who could be quite intimidating when people stopped by without an appointment. She knew how packed the calendar was, and she strove mightily to ensure that our colleague was "protected." People had to get past this executive assistant to get through to our colleague, which was a daunting challenge.

What this loyal person didn't realize was that she was undermining the leader's open-door policy and creating the perception that anyone seeking an unscheduled interaction had to traverse a moat filled with alligators. Upon realizing what was happening, our colleague took her assistant aside and assured her that engaging with others frequently and being available were significant aspects of her job.

What Are the Structural Elements of *Seduction of the Leader*?

It is essential for leaders to be aware of how the structure of an organization—the lines and boxes—can play a powerful role in bringing on seduction. The structure of the office of the president, of a senior cabinet, or of an executive operating committee determines how information flows, whether optimally or not.

Having an efficient and effective office and a solid senior-team structure is essential to the functioning of a president or a CEO. But within that structure, two roles— those of chief of staff and executive vice president—frequently play a powerful role in fostering *seduction of the leader*.

Chiefs of Staff

Many presidents and CEO's are fortunate enough to have a chief of staff. This person can help them manage the pace and complexity of a dynamic organization. A chief of staff who consistently shields a senior leader from challenging or time-consuming individuals, however, may be inviting peril. If this person controls information too thoroughly—whether by breaking it into manageable chunks, translating conversations and synthesizing data inaccurately, or providing summaries or headlines instead of stories—much vital data may be lost.

One of us was sought out by a new president to assist her in establishing a plan for the first 90 days that would lead into a three-year strategic plan. Her chief of staff, having a long history with the university, was to play a critical role in crafting the plan. It was clear from the start that the chief of staff believed that it was his job to protect the president from the clutter and static of the campus so that the president could adapt to her new role. Although the consultant strongly discouraged the chief of staff from taking this approach, he persisted in "protecting" the president during the president's first year.

But the president didn't need protection; she needed connection. In that first year, she should have built the relational capital necessary for her to lead. You can only do that by meeting with people, getting to know them, and— most importantly— listening to them. This means that you *have* to be visible and accessible to your people.

Unfortunately, the president quickly became isolated from campus stakeholders, especially faculty, and problems began to emerge. People mumbled about the lack of communication and accessibility. She earned the dubious moniker "Casper," as in the friendly ghost. Problems grew, but the president was unaware of their intensity, complexity, and nuance. She hadn't been told of the real situation by her chief of staff. So when a complex tangle of issues came to a head, the president was unprepared and overwhelmed. It seemed that problems were emerging from everywhere. Thus, she was ill served by a well-intentioned but ineffective chief of staff.

Do you have structural barriers in your organization? Can your people gain access to you regularly? Is it hard or easy to talk with you? Do you have well meaning "protectors" around you? If so, it's time to make those structures more permeable.

Executive Vice Presidents

Large, complex organizations often have an executive vice president. This person's main responsibilities include managing the CEO's or president's workload, keeping the senior team functioning, crafting the organizational agenda, paying attention to the politics of the place, and moving the big stuff forward. This is an important and challenging job. When done well, it offers substantial benefits to the senior leader.

The most successful executive vice presidents are great listeners and tremendous facilitators who help steer their organizations with intelligence and integrity. However, many executive vice presidents employ a practice at their leader's behest that promotes seduction: they hold private meetings with senior team members. At these meetings, the executive vice president is briefed on the status of projects, key talent, budgetary items, and other important issues. This not only prevents information from getting through to the top leader, but it also gives executive vice presidents a high degree of decision-making authority. This can influence the strategic agenda in powerful ways, potentially steering it away from the senior leader's agenda.

The practice of having executive vice presidents hold one-to-one status meetings can also cause problems for the senior team members. Not having the input of the top leader can set them in the wrong direction or make aspects of their work fail to meet the leader's expectations. In addition, because they aren't meeting with the entire senior team at once, members will lack the advantages of a more holistic organizational view and may fail to see how their actions impact others on the team. Instead, they may operate from within their own towers and may view events through a single lens, such as finance, technology, marketing, or clinical research. This will limit the quality of decision-making, inhibit camaraderie, and stifle mutual support and opportunities for cross-boundary innovation. A sense of ownership for an entire institution and therefore shared accountability will be missing.

This can be addressed partly through periodic meetings of the whole senior team with the executive vice president and the president. Ideally, robust and open conversations about the organization's challenges and opportunities will occur; information will be shared more broadly; and everyone will be more informed. This can only help the top leader and minimize the seduction dynamic.

Proven Strategies to Counter *Seduction of the Leader*

As you can see, strong currents are working against you gaining access to vital information. The seduction of the leader dynamic is always present. But these destructive currents aren't unchangeable; they can be reversed when you build new channels through which communication and feedback can flow. You can promote a culture of candor within your organization. We counsel you to use a range of strategies that foster new behavioral norms.

This is a given: if you have power and influence, you will be working against a tide of reticence when it comes to gaining access to information that sheds a negative light on you, those around you, or your institution. We often tell leaders, "If you're not getting information or feedback on a regular basis that is uncomfortable for you, go seek it out." This requires going beyond the collegial, "How are things going?" or "Let me know if there's anything I need to do."

We cannot stress enough that you have to be *proactive* in encouraging and rewarding behavior that fosters a climate of candor and transparency. If others around you are not pushing back on your ideas, sharing different perspectives, and asking the tough questions, it's very likely that you are being seduced. To counter this, we advise you to enact strategies that create permeable boundaries—permeable enough to allow information and feedback to readily get through. Here are nine powerful strategies that we recommend:

Strategy 1: Use a 360° Feedback Process

In this process, you periodically (about every two years) seek anonymous feedback from others. This is a risky endeavor because the feedback can reveal both wonderful *and* uncomfortable things about leadership effectiveness. For a description of this process, refer to pages 23-24.

Strategy 2: Obtain Feedback with a Leadership Audit

The *leadership audit* is a tool that we created several years ago. It is less rigorous than a 360° process, but can be just as powerful, and provides a quicker, simpler means of obtaining anonymous feedback about how others perceive you. It is essential that a *trusted third party*—such as the human resources department or a trusted external consultant—collect this anonymous data, organize it, and create reports for the leader.

To begin the process, you'll create a set of four to five questions that are of interest to you and distribute them to selected people who know you well. You might want to include questions such as these:

1. What are three things I do well as a leader?

2. What is one thing I could improve upon as a leader?

3. What is one thing I can do to ensure that we continue to improve as a team?

4. What is one piece of advice you can give me that would further enhance my effectiveness?

5. What information might I not already know that is important for me to know and that would improve my effectiveness as a leader?

Keep the list of questions short and sweet. Do not overcomplicate the process. Following these further tips will help you choose your participants and manage feedback wisely:

1. Make sure you solicit answers from at least ten people. If your group is smaller, you won't gain enough data.

2. Seek a balanced perspective by asking a diverse range of people for feedback; don't pick only people who are big fans of yours or only folks with whom you have difficulty.

3. Ensure anonymity for participants. Otherwise, you won't get honest feedback.

4. Make sure that the survey results go to a trusted third party; do not have people send their answers to you. If you can't do this, don't undertake the process.

5. Ask that trusted third party to compile the results, and then meet with that third party to discuss the results.

6. Review the results with more than one person so that you'll benefit from different perspectives on your data. For example, in addition to the person that compiles the data for you, you may share the results with a trusted peer, a mentor, or an external consultant.

STRATEGIC NOTE

You will see that we recommend ensuring people's anonymity. This is essential. Don't assume that people will be open and honest with you because they are nice and ethical. The seduction dynamic is very powerful and pervasive, so anonymous processes give you the best chance of getting the honest information you need.

The answers to a set of thoughtful questions will give you critical and practical information of the sort that leaders rarely receive. Once again, these processes will take real courage on your part, but the benefits can be powerful.

And the benefits will go beyond what you absorb from the feedback when you communicate something back to the people who have taken part. This is a critical component because it demonstrates that you appreciate the time and attention people have invested in the process. You can communicate back in a small meeting with the folks who answered the survey or in one-to-one conversations. Keep the conversation brief (no longer than fifteen minutes), and share what you learned from the feedback in broad strokes to let people know what you gained. Here are some examples of things we've seen people learn through the process and communicate in follow-up meetings:

- I learned that it would be useful for me to be more visible.

- People would like to have quarterly town hall meetings to build a greater sense of community.

- The weekly blog I started to use this year seems to be working well.

- Many people see me as hardworking, fair, and trustworthy.

- I could be more open about the rationale behind the decisions I make.

- I need to improve my listening skills.

However, the process doesn't end with taking in the feedback and sharing what you've learned. Your next crucial step is to follow up on what you've learned—to do something visibly meaningful with the information. You may not be able to respond to everyone's advice, but you can certainly respond to one or two key themes that emerged (such as a need for better listening skills). If people believe that their feedback is truly informing your thinking and actions, they will continue to provide it. If they don't see evidence that you've been affected, you can bet that they won't be so forthcoming next time.

Strategy 3: Create Forums for Dialogue

Leaders determine who gets heard. Never forget this. You must be disciplined and proactive in your efforts to hear perspectives from multiple layers within your organization. People may not be inclined to come to you, especially if you are high up in the hierarchy; *you must go to them.* You must be intentional about being visible and available to your people. Staying trapped in your office or spending large periods away from the office will stifle the voices you need to hear.

Many of the most effective senior leaders with whom we've worked walk around their company's facilities or their campus regularly. They have lunch in the cafeteria frequently, ride the elevators, exercise in the corporate fitness center, or drop in at various departments or office locations—to chat, not to observe. This is a very smart way to function as a leader. If people know that you have lunch in the cafeteria every Friday, they will begin to show up and talk with you. Folks rarely approach strangers, so we encourage you not to be one.

By becoming a familiar presence, you will have access to people's concerns, questions, and aspirations, which helps reduce the seduction dynamic.

Being accessible does not require high levels of orchestration. The most effective leaders we've seen simply meet with people. They host breakfasts or lunches with five to eight employees or faculty members at a time to discuss corporate or institutional issues, faculty concerns, organizational culture, and the "word on the street." They are strategic in ensuring that different departments and different levels of the organization are represented at these get-togethers. Even contractors and adjunct faculty are invited periodically because their perspectives are different and often very helpful.

Simple framing devices such as these will typically suffice for such discussions:

1. What are we doing well as an organization?

2. What are we doing as an organization that needs improvement and needs my attention as a leader?

These forums provide leaders with feedback about organizational and employee life. We recommend that you include someone who is known as a curmudgeon in your conversations. In our experience, these individuals are often quite gifted at speaking truth to power. We caution against inviting deep cynics (individuals who are angry and hopeless), as they can be adept at taking what could be a productive dialogue down a rabbit hole quickly.

Remember during such conversations to approach them with curiosity and stay curious. Your goal is to understand what people are thinking and feeling, not to get caught in a debate. Statements like "Tell me more about that," "Help me understand your thinking," and "This is what I'm hearing, am I on track?" encourage participation and dialogue and show respect to the participants.

Strategy 4: Hold One-on-One Touchpoint Meetings

Many senior leaders are externally focused. They engage in global travel, lobbying efforts, closing sales meetings, and so on and can easily get disconnected from their organization and senior team. Given that their external responsibilities will not change, how can they still maintain vital connections and get access to strategic information?

We have helped create one-on-one touch-point meetings for several senior leaders who are almost always on the road. We suggest that these one-on-one meetings be conducted quarterly, if possible, so that they will maintain meaning and currency.

Here is the process for a one-on-one touch-point meeting. The senior leader distributes a small set of focus questions prior to meeting individually with team members. This ensures that team members can come prepared with thoughtful answers. It's most critical that the senior leader clearly communicates that these meetings are intentional opportunities for sharing the good, the bad, and the ugly. If team members believe that a leader wants to hear the real deal and that there is no need to fear retribution, they will provide a gold mine of information.

Here are suggested questions with which to frame one-on-one touch-point meetings:

1. What accomplishments are you most proud of?

2. What challenges are you currently facing and how can I help?

3. What is happening in your part of the organization that is important for me to know about?

4. Are there things you see happening across the organization that I might not be aware of?

5. What is one piece of advice you have for me that would help me in my role as a leader?

As you can see, the inquiries don't need to be complicated. The right handful of questions can provide much of the critical information you need to get a sense of the organization's climate, its pressing issues, and ways you might adjust your manner of leading to achieve greater impact. The frequent physical distance of an externally focused leader can add mightily to the seduction dynamic, but by being proactive with this process, you can minimize the damage.

Strategy 5: Conduct Skip-Level Meetings

One of the best ways for you to learn what's happening in your organization is to meet with the people who report to your direct reports. There is some risk attached to this, because your direct reports might feel that you are stepping into their territory. But you can allay any potential for anxiety by communicating honestly with them about your reasons, saying that these conversations are not about their effectiveness but about you remaining connected to the organization.

These skip-level meetings are intended to make people working in the next layer down feel comfortable providing you with information that will make you smarter about what's going on throughout the organization. If you're able to create a fair amount of trust and thus to help people feel safe, these meetings will be great information sources for you. If you're in a low-trust environment, however, this practice might not work, because people might be fearful and thus won't share openly.

Here are some suggestions to make your skip-level meetings successful:

1. Let people know ahead of time that you want to meet with them and why.

2. Send them a short list of questions you would like them to think about ahead of the meetings. For example:

    How would you describe communication in your area of responsibility?

    What challenges are you currently facing? What's working well?

Do you have a piece of advice for me that would help me in my leadership role?

What's one thing we need to change in order to thrive in the future?

3. Let them know that your conversations will be confidential.

4. Keep the conversations casual, and meet people where they work; do not summon them to your office.

5. Let folks know that you have about thirty minutes to have a conversation. This creates an expected start and finish to the meeting.

6. After all of the meetings are completed, communicate back a few of the themes that arose. For example:

   I learned that we need to share more information about the strategic plan going forward.

   People want to engage in more cross-boundary information-sharing. Folks want me to be more visible and available.

7. Be sure to share these themes with your direct reports first. This will show your respect for them and will prevent any uncomfortable surprises.

If you can do this process several times throughout the year, skip-level meetings will become a normal practice and be less threatening for everyone, including you. Over time, we've seen leaders share their own leadership challenges in these meetings, and we've seen others share their perspectives and advice openly with leaders. Leaders have almost always been surprised and grateful about the quality of ideas shared.

Strategy 6: Evaluate Your Meeting Forums

Millions of meetings are conducted daily throughout the world's organizations, but the majority are poorly run and predictably mediocre. If you lead, facilitate, or conduct meetings in your organization, one of the most useful things you can do is to ask attendees to periodically evaluate the effectiveness of your meetings in an anonymous format. This will give you the information you need to improve the quality of your meetings going forward. It will also help encourage a climate of candor as people experience the efficacy of this process.

---

5 MEETING EVALUATION QUESTIONS

1. **Given the purposes of this meeting, how effective was it?** (On a scale of 1 to 10, with 1 = not effective, 5 = average, and 10 = very effective)

2. **How involved did you feel in the meeting?** (On a scale of 1 to 10, with 1 = not valued, 5 = average, and 10 = very valued)

3. **What did you like most about the meeting?**

4. **What did you like least about the meeting?**

5. **What other comments, suggestions, or advice do you have that might make our meetings even better?**

This simple idea is powerful. It communicates once again that you are interested in the opinions of others, that soliciting and giving feedback are normal things to do, and that you are open to learning and improving. Everyone has opinions about the meetings they participate in; you need only to create the opportunity and the vehicle for sharing those opinions in a safe way.

You can keep this simple by asking the five questions shown on the facing page after your meetings. Have participants answer them on a survey sheet without identifying themselves. This takes only two to three minutes after a meeting and will be well worth the time.

Share the answers to the survey questions for those who attended the meeting as soon as possible—via email or another method that suits your environment— and listen to and act on the ideas that people have shared. Stay away from the practice of going around the room and openly soliciting advice on how to improve your meetings; people will usually not tell you the truth, *especially* if your meetings are bad.

GET A DEEPER DIAGNOSTIC INTO YOUR MEETINGS

Patrick Sanaghan and Academic Impressions have developed the *Meeting Diagnostic Tool* (MDT), a research-informed instrument to assess the effectiveness of your regular meetings. The MDT looks at four critical elements that either make or break a meeting: 1) discipline and focus; 2) participation and engagement; 3) group dynamics; and 4) practices and protocols.

The good news is that you will now know the bad news—and how to fix it. You can learn more about the MDT at:

https://www.academicimpressions.com/product/meeting-diagnostic-tool-mdt/

Strategy 7: Invite Discomfort

In the classic movie *The Godfather*, the mafia leader Don Corleone stresses to his inner circle of advisers the importance of delivering bad news expeditiously. In essence, he's inviting discomfort. He explains that if he gets the bad news quickly, he has more options for dealing with it. It's essential for you, too, to encourage those around you to share difficult information and emerging problems quickly.

In order to ensure that this will happen, you must recognize and reward the courageous individuals who deliver the difficult news. Doing this will promote a culture of candor and forthrightness. This culture becomes a strategic asset when your people come to you quickly once a problem or challenge begins to emerge.

There are other ways, too, to invite discomfort. Seeking out others who may make you uncomfortable will help you to minimize the potential for comfortable cloning. Leaders often surround themselves with people who are very similar to them. This similarity might be based on gender, race, thinking style (e.g., linear thinkers or more creative thinkers), religious background, educational attainment, or career path (e.g., business-school graduates, those from a development background, or academics).

Such similar individuals are comfortable to us. However, beware of surrounding yourself with comfortable people. Invite the dissenters into your dialogues and discussions. You need people at the table who will offer divergent views and experiences. Seek out diversity, not sameness, if you want to create a stronger organization and become a better leader.

Strategy 8: Involve Others in Your Sense-Making and Decision-Making

We have found that leaders are best served by involving others into their sense-making and decision-making processes. Surprisingly, many leaders are uncomfortable doing this. They assume that just sharing the facts or their final decision is enough. It usually isn't. We encourage leaders to involve others proactively by soliciting their ideas and feedback before making a decision or arriving at a final understanding of a situation. We suggest that you go beyond the perfunctory "Are there any questions?" by declaring that you expect honest feedback—and that you go so far as to invite disagreement and discussion.

Here are some examples of ways you can communicate that will encourage disagreement and other forms of open discussion:

- This is my perspective on the solution and how I arrived at it. *(In our experience, leaders tend not to show others how they arrived at a certain place in their thinking. Almost always, others will appreciate understanding the intellectual journey that you took to get where you are currently.)*

- What am I missing? *(This communicates that you are aware that you may have blind spots and that you want their help to figure out what they might be.)*

- What are some of your ideas that are counter to my current thinking? *(When done authentically, you'll find that people will provide you with differing ideas.)*

- What advice or perspective can you provide to help shape or reshape my thinking? *(This invites people to add value to your ideas. It communicates that you are open to the influence of others.)*

- What have I not accounted for? *(This also communicates that you might have some blind spots and that you are not perfect.)*

- What argument would those who disagree with me make? *(This is a strategic question in many ways. It asks people to think about the flaws in your thinking, helps anticipate possible resistance to the proposed ideas, and makes them think about how others might see it.)*

- What biases of mine might be influencing my perspective? *(This acknowledges that you have biases. If the people know you, they can share where you might be going wrong or might have a blind spot. For example, you might have a strong tendency to see things in financial terms, but the decision you want to make will have a negative impact on company morale.)*

- Why might my proposal not be a good solution? *(This is similar to some questions above but puts out there that you really want to hear why it won't work.)*

- Are there other solutions that would accommodate more agendas and be equally effective? *(By asking this question, you're communicating that you are open to better solutions and ideas.)*

The purpose of these questions is to invite counter views. Why do you need to invite them? Because they won't happen by chance. Active solicitation will prove less fruitful in low-trust environments. However, you can build a sense of trust and openness over time if you persist in seeking disagreement—and if you then act on what you've heard.

As noted earlier, you can create opportunities to experience discomfort by seeking out divergent thinkers, especially those with a negative bent. One of the most successful leaders we've seen often said, "Bring me my critics." Organizational critics are often ignored because of their predictable negativity and their prickly personalities. For them, the glass isn't just half empty; they don't even see that a glass exists! Yet, their ability to look only at what's not working and being tenacious in communicating this to anyone makes them invaluable to leaders.

Why are they invaluable? Because they are often right. Their insights can be informative, even accurate—but their negative reputation derails the credibility of their messages. You may find that they are the only people willing to speak truth to you. Since—as we noted earlier—those surrounding a leader may not give critics an audience with the leader, we highly recommend that you seek them out.

Strategic Note

None of the strategies outlined here should be one-shot deals. Whichever ones you choose to employ, employ them regularly, and make sure you attend carefully to the process and follow through. Sloppiness, inconsistency, or a failure to follow through damages your credibility and invites seduction.

Strategy 9: Make Reflection a Habit

Regular reflection is one of the disciplines of highly effective leaders. Self-awareness gained through personal reflection in the privacy of your own head is a powerful remedy for seduction. Some of the very best leaders we've worked with have kept journals for years, viewing them as strategic assets and key elements in their journeys. We strongly suggest that you, too, find a way to capture what you are experiencing, learning, curious about, or upset with as you travel your path as a leader.

Below are several questions that have been helpful to the best leaders with whom we've worked. We suggest them as starting points—initial guides to capture your thinking.

To make use of this method, schedule a fifteen-minute meeting with yourself *every day* and hold it sacred. Take this time to choose three or four questions that feel most relevant and to answer them. Whenever you're able, review your answers over time, examining them carefully for recurring themes, clues to what lay behind successes or failures, and blind spots.

Achieving this distance from your own reflections and figuring out ways to put what you learn into action can be difficult. A mentor, confidant, or trusted colleague can help you to see what your self-reflection reveals and to apply what you're learning in your day-to-day leadership practice. If you don't have such a person in your professional life, find one.

Here are some questions you can choose from when engaging in self-reflection.

1. What issues or challenges might I be avoiding? Have I invited anyone to challenge me?

2. What am I worried, confused, or anxious about? Have I jumped at solutions today to reduce my anxiety?

3. What assumptions are contributing to the key decisions I've made this week? Are those

assumptions helping me make good decisions? What are my biases, and how are they informing my assumptions?

4. Who have I shown appreciation to or recognized in some way recently? Are there others I've overlooked who deserve such recognition?

5. Who around me may be shielding me from information that I need? How might I invite them to talk with me?

6. What stories am I paying attention to, and which am I ignoring?

7. Who is getting on my nerves or making me uncomfortable? What might I need from that individual?

Choose the questions that you feel comfortable with and that make you reflect more deeply. Setting aside time for this sort of self-reflection isn't easy; all of us can get caught up in the enduring rapids of our lives and find a dozen reasons to blow off this exercise. If you can be disciplined about doing this self-reflection, however, you'll develop more self-awareness, which can help neutralize the seduction dynamic.

Closing Thoughts

One of the toughest jobs you may ever have as a leader is the job of gaining access to a full range of perspectives. This full range is necessary to optimize how you run your business. In our many years of experience, we have come to understand that most people just don't naturally share bad news. The seduction of the leader is always present.

But you need to hear all kinds of news. You can deal with what you know about. Discovering what you don't know about should be your constant pursuit.

In writing this chapter, our first objective was to describe the *seduction of the leader*— what it looks like, how prevalent it is, and the main interpersonal and structural dynamics that drive it. Our second objective was to share proven strategies for neutralizing or overturning it. We've provided you with nine such strategies, and they all have these qualities in common:

1. They invite information.

2. They demand listening.

3. They require a thoughtful response.

4. They call for consistent application.

5. They involve courage on your part.

All of these five qualities are challenging. In our experience, the most effective leaders understand deeply the challenges associated with tapping into their people's full range of experience, knowledge, and views; effective leaders tap these resources anyway. We've had the privilege of working with a handful of them to test and refine the set of approaches we've shared here. These approaches will prove useful to you—if you aspire to have those around you tell you what's *really* going on.

CHAPTER 3: MICROMANAGEMENT —IS IT INCURABLE?

Overview

In his book, *My Way or The Highway* (Chambers, 2004), Harry E. Chambers cites a survey of several hundred managers and employees in which 79% of those surveyed reported that they had experienced micromanagement with their current or past managers.

This figure resonates with my own experience in teaching over a hundred leadership development programs in higher education over the years. Whenever I ask participants if they have ever worked for a micromanager in the course of their careers, between 80-90% raise their hands. When I ask how many enjoyed the experience or found it beneficial, no hands are raised.

If so many have experienced micromanagement and find it unhelpful, why does micromanaging persist?

Micromanaging is an easy habit to identify in others but a very difficult habit to break in ourselves. It takes patience, persistence, and mindfulness, and even then, it is a long shot. By identifying what makes a micromanager, it is possible to understand how to break the habit. Considering the negative impact and toxic environment that micromanaging creates, it is well worth the effort

(Blackney, 2013; Barnes, 2015; Chambers, 2004; Ivy, 2014; Buckley, 2014).

MICROMANAGEMENT: DEFINITIONS

"To direct or control in a detailed, often meddlesome manner."

- *The Free Dictionary*

"To manage especially with excessive control or attention to details."

- *Merriam Webster*

What Does a Micromanager Look Like?

Several researchers have identified some of the reasons why people micromanage; these perspectives can be a useful framework for understanding the complex dynamics behind this noxious management style (Chambers, 2004; Ashkenas, 2011; Chatman 2011). Here is what they have found.

Micromanagers are using a skill set that has worked for them in the past.

Often, micromanagers begin as staff who have developed effective "operational" skills and are good at achieving goals, managing budgets, and solving problems. This technical or functional expertise enables them to be promoted because they "get stuff done." However, as managers ascend the career ladder, they are expected to be more strategic, develop their people, and delegate more, which is a skill set that is distinct and often opposite to their operational ability. They overcorrect by trying to do more of the same, by trying to maintain control over everything. They lack the flexibility and agility to shift their leadership behaviors and become more effective.

Micromanagers fear negative outcomes.

Micromanagers are motivated by fear of failure, public embarrassment, being left out of the information loop, or fear of not knowing what is going on with people. Though this negative fear doesn't go away, the power of it can diminish over time (Chambers, 2004; White, 2010).

Micromanagers fear being uninformed.

Often, micromanagers strongly believe that operational details are important to hold onto. They fear losing touch with "the real stuff," and they overcompensate by seeking lots of information. They ask for reports to keep them updated, and they attend too many meetings, all in a drive to know, in detail, what's going on.

This causes confusion because staff do not understand the rationale behind creating extra reports, or why a manager is attending meetings they probably don't need to be involved with.

Micromanagers take a "my way or the highway" approach.

Micromanagers like to exercise raw power and often assert their authority simply because they can (Chambers, 2004;

Manzoni, 2002; Chatman, 2011). They see compromise as a weakness and see stubbornness as strength. They rarely back off from a position they have taken. Under real stress, they adopt a "my way or the highway" approach (Chambers, 2004; White, 2010), and the actual 'what' and 'why' of the situation become irrelevant. Taking on a micromanager is not for the faint of heart, and a direct, confrontational approach, unless you have considerable power yourself, is not the way to go.

Micromanagers distrust the judgment of others.

They tend to be poor listeners because they think they already know how things should be done. They are not interested in others' advice, experience, or perspective. They rarely clarify the rules by which decisions will be made, and they rarely give others meaningful authority. This creates an "approval" process wherein people have to continually check in with the micromanager before moving forward. This, in turn, creates bottlenecks because everything has to cross the micromanager's desk before it can move to the next step.

Micromanagers cannot delegate effectively because:

- They do not trust others to do quality work.

- They believe they are the only ones who can do the work properly.

- If they *do* delegate, they will pull back at the first hint of trouble. Instead of seeing the delegation process as a way to develop others, they rush in to save the day.

- They rarely delegate interesting or important assignments, but prefer to dump only trivial and boring work.

Micromanagers thrive on a sense of urgency.

The control of time is one of the most intense drivers for micromanagers. They constantly interrupt people's work with intrusive check-ins and trivial questions: Are they on time? Are they doing personal work at their desks? Are they playing by all the rules and procedures? These interruptions demoralize people because they are so unnecessary and are a waste of their time.

Micromanagers also create unrealistic deadlines, which puts a time pressure on almost everything and creates a false sense of urgency both on priorities *and* trivial matters.

Micromanagers thrive in a crisis because they are most happy when they can declare an "emergency" and take over. They thrive on stress; they need to control; and they prefer to be the only one who can take care of the situation. Perversely, this *does not* mean that they are effective in a crisis.

The Negative Impact of Micromanagers

Micromanagers can have a pervasive and negative impact on an organization's effectiveness and productivity. They can create a caustic campus climate and take away far more than they ever contribute. The challenge with micromanagers is that they apply the same level of scrutiny, attention to detail, and control to *every task*, whether it is a priority or not (Chambers, 2004; Maignan Wilkins, 2014). This causes undue stress for their direct reports, who can no longer prioritize their own work because *everything is important.*

We are not trying to be mean here, but we want to be as direct and honest as we can: *Micromanagers cause much more harm than good.*

The following is an informal snapshot of the research confirming the negative impact of micromanagers:

1. They create unnecessary bottlenecks with over-monitoring and approval processes (Chambers, 2004; Ivy, 2014; Mayhew).

2. They stifle the creativity and initiative of their employees (Chambers, 2004; Blackney, 2013; Ivy, 2014; Parks, 2015).

3. They fail to develop their people (Chambers, 2004; White, 2010).

4. This reduces the quality of work produced (Collins & Collins, 2002; Chambers, 2004; Blackney, 2013; Barnes, 2015).

5. In turn, employee morale suffers (Chambers, 2004; Wilkens, 2014; Parks, 2015).

6. And employees are more disengaged in the workplace (Bielaszka-DuVernay, 2008; Heiman, 2010; Blackney, 2013; Parks, 2015).

7. All of this results in high employee turnover (Collins & Collins, 2002; Chamber, 2004; (Blackney, 2013; Mayhew).

In short, not a pretty picture.

> "Micromanagement does not add value to individuals or processes. Regardless of the intent, the results are subtraction not addition."—*Chambers, 2004*

It's important to note that micromanagement isn't usually malicious in nature. There is some limited research that indicates that micromanagers might not understand the negative impact they have on their people and the work environment, and may truly believe that they are just practicing good management (Chambers, 2004; Stell, 2006). Often, they only get a picture of their negative impact when they are involved in an anonymous, 360° feedback process. I have had several debriefs with senior micromanagers who were very surprised to learn that they were perceived as annoying, aggravating, and ineffective.

At the very least, this kind of valuable feedback and information can create a "choice point" for the micromanaging leader. Once they fully realize their impact, they can choose to act differently, but the journey toward new behaviors will be a difficult one. (Later in this chapter, we'll share a few practical strategies for that journey.)

Is Micromanaging Always Bad?

Obviously, there are specific times when a *little* micromanaging can be helpful. These are situation-specific and should not be taken to suggest that micromanagement can be productive as a consistent approach to leading an organization effectively and efficiently (Spolsky, 2009; Riordan, 2009). These situations include:

1. **When a new person comes on board.** In the case of a new addition to an existing team, task force, or group, it is almost always helpful to monitor their activities closely until they under-

stand the lay of the land, are clear about their responsibilities, and have developed the relational network to get things done. This is usually somewhere between 30 and 90 days. If the new person is still being monitored closely after that 90-day period, this is probably a case of either a poor hire or an emerging habit of micromanaging.

2. **When an organizational strategy is changing dramatically** (Riordan, 2009). In this kind of transition, there is a lot of confusion and complexity. Close attention and monitoring during this time is expected and often needed. People need to understand the rationale behind the new strategy and its implications for their daily work. Making that pivotal connection is important for people; close supervision, answering questions, and closely monitoring behaviors and activities is appropriate. Once again, the 30 to 90 day rule is a helpful guideline. People need to know that this "mini"-micromanaging is a temporary situation.

3. **An important project flounders and begins to fail.** In this situation, closer attention can be a constructive approach until things are turned around. Paying close attention to results and determining why things aren't working well will take time and persistence on the manager's part. Conducting a careful and detailed After Action Report (AAR) or a Post Mortem also identifies lessons learned.

The bottom line here is that there are some times during which micromanaging can be a helpful but *temporary* approach to managing others (Riordan, 2009; Spolsky, 2009; Collins & Collins, 2002).

Advice for Dealing with a Micromanaging Boss

"The worst thing you can do when facing micromanagement is nothing."

—*Chambers, 2004*

In this section, we'll present a brief, informal case study and seven concrete strategies for employees.

CASE STUDY: THE MICROMANAGING EVP

I once worked with the executive vice president of a large Research I university. This leader had served as a high-ranking officer in the military and obtained an electrical engineering Ph.D. during his 25 years of service. He was highly intelligent, dedicated, action-oriented, and one of the great micromanagers of all time. His work ethic and his attention to detail, *every* detail, had enabled him to move up the military ranks quickly, because he got things done. The traditional hierarchy of the military tolerated and even enabled his attention to detail and his command-and-control style.

He looked like the right fit for an EVP for a complex and somewhat disorganized campus. Initially, he met with great success. He established standing meetings with priority stakeholders, created protocols for communication and coordination between offices, organized the president's cabinet, and started to move things along at a quick pace.

CASE STUDY: THE MICROMANAGING EVP, CONTINUED

But after about six months, things started to change. People complained about too many standing meetings during which the EVP conducted monologues instead of dialogues with staff. Because the EVP felt he should be involved in almost everything, the pipeline of actions and decisions slowed, bottlenecks emerged, and people were unsure about what they could and couldn't do without his permission.

The president asked for some help with this situation because she was in a bind. She didn't want to lose this leader, but she also didn't think he would be open to feedback—and her people were complaining loudly. I met with the EVP several times over a month, and had very open discussions about his micromanaging style.

He knew that he had to change, but didn't know how. The very skills that had helped him reach this prestigious leadership position were not helping him in his current role. He didn't want to fail in this new role, so he was very motivated to change at least *some* things.

My discussions with him revealed that in the beginning of his military career, he had been staffed by an outstanding sergeant who was excellent about all the details and who was deeply trusted. This had enabled the leader to focus on more important and strategic issues, because "Sarge" had his back. With this great support, he was able to advance to higher positions and responsibilities. This made it clear what was needed in the current situation: We had to find another "Sarge."

Working with HR, we identified an administrative assistant who was recognized throughout her division as a "detail" person, a great organizer, and who was very pleasant to work with. When contacted about a possible job transfer, she was both interested—because working with an EVP had great status attached to it—and reluctant—because this EVP's reputation was well known throughout the campus.

We agreed to a meeting, and after several conversations, we created some strategies we hoped would prove helpful in this transition process. The administrative assistant was assured that if things did not work out she could go back to her former division (this was a key part of the agreement). Together, we established a set of protocols that would keep the EVP informed and in touch with many of his areas of responsibility.

The administrative assistant:

- Scheduled a twice weekly "scorecard" meeting with the EVP, where the status of projects would be updated using an agreed-upon scoring system.

- Created one-page formats for ongoing reports and met with the EVP's direct reports to communicate what needed to be included in these reports.

- Established two important ground rules: 1) She would bring "bad" news as fast as possible, *with no repercussions*, and 2) she would have the authority to push back when she thought the EVP was micromanaging too much. (This was the one ground rule that was the "game changer.")

> **CASE STUDY: THE MICROMANAGING EVP, CONTINUED**
>
> - Attended all of the EVP's meetings for a month. She then provided a rigorous review of how effective the meetings were and if they were worth his time and attention. Although the EVP initially opposed changes to his schedule, his meeting attendance was soon reduced by 40%.
>
> Over a year, the EVP and the assistant worked through these practices, and the EVP's management style changed dramatically. His staff were happy, the president was happy, and things started to move forward. The administrative assistant was the right person at the right time, with the right skill set and with the emotional intelligence needed. Everyone learned that this kind of trusted support can work with a micromanager.

7 Strategies to Deal with a Micromanager

First, as an employee, do a self-assessment. It is important for employees to reflect on their own work practices and production: Are you completing quality work? Are deadlines being met? Do you start and attend meetings on time? Do you add value in meaningful and visible ways? (Ganeshan-Singh, 2014)

These can seem like risky questions because in assessing these areas, you may feel you are supplying the micromanager with "ammunition" to apply more control, establish tighter deadlines, and ask for more points of approval in the process. This self-assessment is nevertheless crucial. As an employee, you need to fix any inefficient areas, acknowledging them and committing to improve. You need to let the micromanager know that you realize there are areas to improve and that you are committed to working on them. Micromanagers will be more likely to loosen some of the controls if they see real progress.

Once you have committed to that, use these 7 key strategies to mitigate the negative impact of micromanagement on your work:

1. **Keep good records:** This is important because micromanagers often forget what directions they have given and what commitments they have made. After a meeting, capture the essence of the conversation along with any agreed-upon actions to take, and share this written synopsis with the manager. This is an opportunity to both set expectations and clear up any confusion. This is not meant to be a "gotcha" to show them they are wrong, as this will only aggravate them. It is meant to be sensible recordkeeping that keeps people on the same page.

2. **Confirm deadlines:** Often micromanagers establish unrealistic deadlines because they do not know how much work is actually invested in projects. Be proactive here and create a realistic deadline based on your experience, and give specific reasons for the timeframe. It is also helpful to suggest "mini" deadlines as an opportunity to check in with the micromanager so that you can keep them updated along the way.

3. **Prioritize the work:** Micromanagers often have a difficult time with prioritization. Provide a rationale for your priorities (e.g., the complexity or

urgency) so that these have some weight. If the micromanager gives you a new assignment, re-prioritize with them to make sure all assignments are done well and on time.

4. **Request "update" meetings:** Keep ahead of a micromanager and don't wait to be asked for updates on work projects. Ask for a specific time during the week to share progress and identify challenges. Be ready to receive advice, especially around the challenges encountered. Focus on the successes to balance their tendency to focus on the problems.

5. **Identify people who can work with the micromanaging boss:** There might be people in your office who have learned how to manage the micromanager. Pinpoint the strategies they use to deal with micromanaging behaviors. Are there things you can adopt that will be helpful?

6. **Be diligent:** Be on time for meetings, come prepared for update meetings, show up for work on time, and use technology appropriately (no personal business). Micromanagers are fond of catching people bending the rules. Don't get on their radar screen.

7. **Establish working agreements:** Micromanagers like structure and predictability, so it is important to provide them with this. Like most leaders, they find "surprises" distasteful, and as micromanagers, they tend to overreact to surprises.

   - Ask for a weekly (if not daily) progress report meeting. Be prepared at this meeting and keep the manager apprised of the work being accomplished. This is never a casual check-in; it is a serious conversation that will provide them with the information they crave and possibly build their confidence in you.

- Have a ground rule: "Report bad news ASAP." Commit to sharing emerging problems and challenges quickly. Prevent the big surprises; this will build trust.

- Have an agreed upon "scorecard" that is visible, easy to understand, and maintained with a simple rubric. One option is a list of priority projects with a color code:

Green = project is progressing well

Yellow = project is moving along with some "glitches"

Red = project is in trouble

Articulate why the red projects are in trouble. Offer some possible solutions for the glitches in the yellow projects. Micromanagers will prefer to focus solely on the problems because that will stimulate their anxiety, so balance by also reviewing the green projects that show that progress is being made.

Advice for Micromanagers

In this section, we'll present a brief, informal case study and nine concrete strategies for managers.

CASE STUDY: THE MICROMANAGING PRESIDENT

Several years ago, I worked with a well-known academic who became president on a campus that was treading water. Retention was poor, graduation rates were plummeting, fundraising was almost non-existent, and faculty excellence was dwindling. In short, not a pretty picture.

This president's style involved being a "nice micromanager." He knew all the details, monitored everything closely, wrote numerous reports and memos, and called endless meetings to create solutions to the challenges the campus was facing. He moved the ball forward carefully and tenaciously, one small step at a time. Over time, the campus began to move forward, too, and after five years was in much better shape, mostly due to his great efforts.

Then problems began to emerge. The "nice micromanager" style that created the initial success wasn't working anymore, and he didn't know how to change his behavior to meet the new challenges and opportunities that were present. Two of his VP's left within an academic year, and in exit interviews relayed that they didn't feel they'd had the chance to actually spread their wings and lead.

Everything went through the president's desk, and that desk was very full. They wanted to make a difference, but felt that they couldn't make one under this president.

The president undertook a 360° feedback process after a close friend and fellow president suggested it. The results were startling and surprising to him. He was stunned that although people appreciated his great contributions, they didn't like his leadership style at all.

> ## CASE STUDY: THE MICROMANAGING PRESIDENT, CONT.
>
> People wanted him to delegate the authority to lead. They wanted clarity on the rules by which decisions would be made. They wanted freedom within their units and an end to endless meetings.
>
> I suggested that the president work with a local executive coach I knew well, who could help him navigate the difficult journey towards letting go. He needed someone he trusted, and because he was a forceful character, he also needed someone who was strong enough to push back.
>
> Over the course of a year, he learned to clarify the decision rules for his staff so that they knew their scope of authority. In the process, he cut his meetings in half. Those were two very difficult steps for him, but his natural persistence worked in his favor. Around six months into the process, he gathered anonymous feedback about how he was doing and received an overwhelmingly positive response. This motivated him to work on a couple more things (not everything at once), and he moved slowly and steadily towards being less controlling. He communicated that the urge to clamp down and take over things was still there, but he realized that giving in to that urge would not serve his people well.

In the case study above, the president was someone who really listened to the feedback he received and, with some strong support, learned how to lead differently. His traditional style had been effective in the earlier circumstances, but as the institution's situation changed, he had to learn how to lead in a more effective and sustainable way. He spent 15 years at this campus and left it in a much better place. He retired as President Emeritus for his great contributions.

His success leaves some clues for other micromanagers:

1. Seek ongoing, anonymous feedback. *(This takes real courage.)*

2. Listen to that feedback even when it hurts. *(It probably will.)*

3. Get support with the leadership journey. *(Never walk alone when trying to change an embedded leadership style.)*

4. To shift your management style, take one or two things on; do not attempt to change everything all at once. *(It simply won't work.)*

5. Take the pulse of how you are doing on a regular basis. This will allow you to do a course correction if needed. *(It will also show your people that giving and receiving feedback is "normal" and appropriate for managers at all levels of the institution, and that you are a committed learner.)*

6. Understand that leading differently is really hard, with no shortcuts, but that in the end, leading differently serves the people and the place well. *(This is a key thing to remember: You are serving the mission of the campus and its people. That mission provides you with a higher purpose that can support difficult, personal change.)*

9 Ways to Micromanage Less

1. Acknowledge the challenge

Acknowledge to your staff that your current style of management might not be as effective as you would like it to be. This will take some courage, but this is an essential message to convey. It is the first step in the "recovery" journey.

2. Ask for feedback

Ask your staff how you can be more helpful and listen to their answers. You might hear answers like:

- Hold fewer meetings.

- Clarify your decision rules (e.g., "When can I move forward with an assignment? What real approvals do I need from you?").

- Instead of interrupting people throughout the day, identify a specific time to review work, ask questions, give advice, and approve progress.

Quarterly, ask the following three simple questions of your people. Make sure their answers are *anonymous*, and ask for as many specifics as possible:

- What do I currently do that helps you?

- What should I stop doing?

- What should I continue to do?

3. Streamline reporting

Request brief (no more than one page) updates that highlight the most important information.

4. Learn to delegate

This is one of the best ways to develop your staff. There are several good books and articles on the delegation process that can help you:

- *How to Delegate Effectively Without Losing Control* by Peter A. Land (Insight, 2006).

- *If You Want It Done Right, You Don't Have To Do It By Yourself* by Donna M. Genett (Quill Driver Books, 2004).

- *The Busy Manager's Guide to Delegation* by Richard A. Luecke and Perry McIntosh (AMACOM, 2009).

5. Learn to differentiate the trivial from the important

Identify the consistent and repetitive tasks and loosen your control of those. Focus on the priority projects, not the mundane activities. As it has been said, "Don't major in the minors." Focus your time and attention on the most important things, not everything. (Note: You will probably need help with this.)

6. Invest in executive coaching

You don't need to correct your micromanaging behaviors by yourself. With a good coach, you will be able to create a *realistic* game plan to minimize your micromanagement. This is key – do not attempt to go cold turkey, committing to quit micromanaging all together. Start with one micromanaging behavior (e.g., poor delegation, fuzzy decision rules, calling too many meetings, or going overboard on approvals) and tackle that one thing with a coach, building a plan to improve it. Patience, persistence, and discipline will be essential. A coach can help you with strategy, moral support, and honest feedback. This is an investment of time and money, but it is an investment worth making.

7. Consider journaling on a consistent basis.

Many leaders have reported that keeping a journal was helpful in their journey toward less micromanagement. Two outcomes usually emerge from journaling:

- By recording how many meetings they hold, how many "approvals" they request, how often they interrupt their people, etc., managers realize how pervasive their micromanagement really is, which is both humbling and disturbing. This rich database can paint a powerful picture of your management "habit."

- You may begin to identify certain themes and trends. You may find that you micromanage certain people more than others. Or you may see that meetings are one-way monologues, not meaningful dialogues. Or you may identify how often your people come back to ask trivial questions or permission to do things.

8. Suggest some "operating agreements"

Establish a ground rule or "operating agreement." After initial success, choose another ground rule or agreement to implement. Take one at a time and improve slowly and persistently.

9. Describe the success you want to see

When delegating an assignment, strive mightily to provide a picture of what that assignment's success will look like. Micromanagers are usually not very good at establishing clear expectations and accountabilities (Chambers, 2004) and this often creates confusion. They live by the adage, "I might not know what I want currently, but I will know it when I see it." From the perspective of your staff, this leaves things quite mysterious and encourages you to "dip into" people's work often. Instead, create a picture with staff so they know what they are trying to achieve.

Adapting your management style is not a journey for the faint of heart. Changing your micromanaging habits and tendencies is a difficult journey to undertake – but the positive impact it will have on your people will be enormous.

AN INFORMAL MICROMANAGEMENT ASSESSMENT

How do you know if you work for a micro-manager? You can use this set of questions as an informal assessment to evaluate your current boss and determine if they are a true micromanager. You can also use it as a self-assessment to better understand your own micromanagement tendencies. All of these questions have been informed by the research on micromanaging (Chambers, 2004; Fracaro, 2007; Stell, 2006; Bielaska-DuVerney, 2008).

1. My manager consistently seeks too much information about what I am working on.

1	2	3	4	5
Strongly Disagree	Disagree	Neutral	Agree	Strongly Agree

2. My manager is an ineffective delegator (e.g., doesn't explain the rationale for an assignment; provide me with challenging assignments; establish good communication protocols; or help prioritize my work).

1	2	3	4	5
Strongly Disagree	Disagree	Neutral	Agree	Strongly Agree

3. Most of the time, my manager tells me what to do and how to do it, rather than empowering me to find the best approach on my own.

1	2	3	4	5
Strongly Disagree	Disagree	Neutral	Agree	Strongly Agree

4. My manager requires a lot of *unnecessary* approvals and check-ins about the assignments I am given (e.g., double checking everything, providing constant advice, not allowing me to move forward, etc.).

1	2	3	4	5
Strongly Disagree	Disagree	Neutral	Agree	Strongly Agree

5. My manager is not a good listener.

1	2	3	4	5
Strongly Disagree	Disagree	Neutral	Agree	Strongly Agree

6. My manager interrupts and disrupts my work too much.

1	2	3	4	5
Strongly Disagree	Disagree	Neutral	Agree	Strongly Agree

7. I do not clearly understand my decision making authority (e.g., what decisions I can make and which ones I can't).

1	2	3	4	5
Strongly Disagree	Disagree	Neutral	Agree	Strongly Agree

8. I believe my manager does not trust me to do good work and make good decisions.

1	2	3	4	5
Strongly Disagree	Disagree	Neutral	Agree	Strongly Agree

9. Often, when my manager gives me work to do, he/she takes it back and does it him/herself.

1	2	3	4	5
Strongly Disagree	Disagree	Neutral	Agree	Strongly Agree

10. People in the office describe my manager as a "micromanager."

1	2	3	4	5
Strongly Disagree	Disagree	Neutral	Agree	Strongly Agree

Assessing Your Boss

Add up your tallied scores and divide by 10. This will give you an average score for the assessment.

If the score = 1-2: Any average below a 2 is great! This usually means you are working for an effective manager who knows how to delegate, provides good communication, lets you actually do your assignments, and clarifies the decision rules. You are fortunate.

If the score = 3: If your average "hovers" around a three, it usually means you are unsure about the micromanaging tendencies of your manager. The three questions to focus on that might clarify your experience with your manager are #6, #8, and #10. Take a closer look at how you responded to each of those three questions on the assessment; this will help clarify how you perceive your boss's management style.

If the score = 4: You work for a micromanager -- but there is hope! Many of the strategies in this chapter can work with a moderate micromanager.

If the score = More than 4.5: You work with a full-blown micromanager, and you are dealing with a very difficult situation indeed. Some of the strategies in this chapter might be effective, but the odds are against you. The keys in this case are to do excellent work, keep them informed about your work and your progress, and be **proactive** in responding to them.

Assessing Yourself

If you use this informal but informed survey as a self-assessment and find that you have strong micromanaging tendencies, you should understand two things:

1. Your micromanaging is ineffective and destructive in the long term. You might achieve some short term results using this management style, but in the end your people will resent you. They will become disengaged, and you will see diminishing returns in the quality of the results they offer.

2. It's time to ask your people what they need from you, how they think you can be a more effective supervisor and manager. If they truly believe that you are committed to changing your behavior and if they trust your intentions, they will be able to suggest some effective protocols and procedures you can use to be more successful.

References

Ashkenas, R. "Why People Micromanage." *Harvard Business Review*, 15 March 2011.

Barnes, L. "The Damaging Effects of Micromanagement." *PA Times*, 31 March 2015. Retrieved from: https://patimes.org/damaging-effects-micromanagement/

Bielaszka-DuVernay, C. "Micromanage at Your Peril." *Harvard Business Review*, 29 February 2008.

Blackney, B. "The Debilitating Effects of Micromanagement." *TB Logical*, 6 August 2013.

Chambers, H.E. *My Way or the Highway: The Micromanagement Survival Guide*. Berrett-Koehler Publishers, 2004.

—. "Surviving the Micromanager: How to succeed with a "my way" boss." *Career-Intelligence.com*, 9 April 2018. Retrieved from: http://career-intelligence.com/surviving-micromanager/

Collins, SK, and KS Collins. "Micromanagement--a Costly Management Style." *Radiology Management*, vol. 24, no.6, 2002.

Fracaro, Kenneth E. "The Consequences of Micromanaging." *Contract Management*, July 2007.

Gallo, Amy. "Stop Being Micromanaged." *Harvard Business Review*, 22 September 2011.

Ganeshan-Singh, Padmaja. "7 Ways to Survive Working for a Micromanager." *PayScale*, 29 October 2014.

Retrieved from: https://www.payscale.com/career-news/2014/10/7-ways-to-survive-working-for-a-micromanaging-boss

Graham Scoll, G. *A Survival Guide for Working with Bad Bosses: Dealing with Bullies, Idiots, Back-Stabbers, And Other Managers from Hell.* AMACOM, 25 November 2005.

Hall, Linda and Kent Lineback. "How to Get Involved Without Micromanaging People." *Harvard Business Review*, 25 March 2011.

Knight, Rebecca. "How to Stop Micromanaging Your Team." *Harvard Business Review*, 21 August 2015.

Maignan Wilkins, Muriel. "Signs That You're A Micromanager." *Harvard Business Review*, 11 November 2014.

Manzoni, J F, and Jean-Louis Barsoux. *The Set-Up-to-Fail Syndrome: How Good Managers Cause Great People to Fail.* Harvard Business School Press, 2002.

Mayhew, R. "Micromanagement's Effects on Employees." *Houston Chronicle.*

Popick, Janine. "Just Say No to Micromanaging." *Inc.*, 29 March 2013.

Rao, Kathleen. *My Boss Is a Jerk: How to Survive and Thrive in a Difficult Work Environment Under the Control of a Bad Boss.* Amazon Digital Services LLC, 2014.

Riordan, C.M. "Sometimes Micromanaging Is Good and Necessary." *Forbes*, 29 July 2009.

Spolsky, J. "When & How to Micromanage." *Inc.*, December 2009.

Stell, R. "Micromanagement Is Mismanagement: Are You a Micromanager?" National Federation of Independent Business, 27 November 2006.

Su, Amy J, and Muriel M. Wilkins. *Own the Room: Discover Your Signature Voice to Master Your Leadership Presence.* Harvard Business Review Press, 2013.

Ivy, T. "The Devastating Consequences of Micro-Management." *Linked Pulse*, 13 November 2014.

White, R.D. "The Micromanagement Disease: Symptoms, Diagnosis, and Cure." *Public Personnel Management,* Vol. 39, 2010, pp. 69-76.

CHAPTER 4:
THE IGNORANCE
OF ARROGANCE

Overview

"Arrogance is the mother of all derailers." - Tim Irwin

The above quote—from Tim Irwin's excellent book, *Derailed: Five Lessons Learned from Catastrophic Failures of Leadership* (2012)—coincides with my experience working with some leaders in higher education. I have had the opportunity to work with hundreds of higher education leaders over the past 25+ years. Nearly all of these leaders have been intelligent, dedicated, honest, and ethical. But on occasion, I have encountered an arrogant leader, and these interactions have been unpleasant and distasteful.

I have witnessed arrogant leaders interrupt others, be sarcastic, belittle people's ideas, and remain closed to any feedback about their ideas or behavior. Many of them were cowards, unwilling to look at the negative impact they had on others. When an arrogant leader holds a senior position, that leader creates a toxic environment that harms the people who work with that leader and the institution.

This chapter will explore:

1. What arrogance looks like in a leader, and how it works;

2. The negative impact on that arrogance on others; and

3. Strategies to adopt when faced with an arrogant leader, which *might* help mitigate their behaviors.

What Does Arrogance Look Like?

Let's consider a few definitions of arrogance:

- "Having an attitude of superiority manifested in an *overbearing* manner or in presumptuous claims or assumptions." – Merriam-Webster Dictionary.

- "Engaging in behavior intended to exaggerate a person's sense of superiority by *disparaging others.*" – Johnson (2010).

- "A state of overbearing pride or self-importance with *contempt for others.*" – Jenks & Steele (2012).

I emphasized specific words above to make a point: Arrogance is not just a healthy dose of confidence or even just a "pompous" or "blustery" personality. Arrogant people demonstrate *contempt* for others and are disparaging and insulting to the people they work with. Additionally, arrogant people are rarely able to arrest their attitudes or behavior; they cannot hide their arrogance or rein in their actions. That is why arrogance damages people, teams, and organizations.

As we unpack the dynamics of arrogant leadership, it will be helpful to identify some of the behaviors that the truly arrogant display on a regular basis. Use the following list of warning behaviors to assess your own actions (many of us are at least slightly guilty of some of these behaviors), as well as those of subordinates, peers, and emerging leaders at your organization. If we can recognize the warning behaviors, we might be able to intervene to provide strong support and coaching before the arrogant leader fails or derails.

1. Arrogant leaders are often late for meetings

Arrogant leaders believe their time is more valuable than others', and they rarely apologize for being late. This often fosters resentment in others who have arrived well-prepared to start the discussion and who have had to delay the conversation until the arrogant leader's eventual arrival. This doesn't only waste time; it is disrespectful. The impact is especially acute when the arrogant leader holds a senior position, because it is more likely that colleagues will be left in a holding pattern until the leader's arrival.

2. Arrogant leaders don't often ask questions

In fact, they think they already have the answers. Why ask questions when you already know what needs to be done? When they do ask questions during team or group discussions, these are often tinged with sarcasm: "Isn't it *obvious* that Option #3 is the way to go?" or "Could we move on, please? We are beating this item to death."

They may also ask questions in such a way as to make others look unintelligent: "Does anyone *else* think this is a good solution? I didn't think so. It seems very limited to me." Or: "What is your rationale for this recommendation? It seems silly to me." Colleagues often react viscerally to the edge that they hear in such questions, and the discussion can turn sour and contentious. The team may even close down real and open discussion quickly, because people don't want to be the target of a sarcastic or cutting remark. Arrogant leaders create a negative meeting culture in which discussions remain limited, and no one looks forward to them.

3. Arrogant leaders may offer condescending gestures

For example, an arrogant leader who wears glasses may peer over their lenses or literally look down their nose at others. They may roll their eyes to indicate exasperation with the discussion, tap a pen on the table to remind others to "move along," or shuffle papers loudly. They are aware that they are sending an implicit message to others, but they usually don't care about the offense others may feel; they just hope others will get the point. Despite their lack of empathy, however, if they encounter a colleague who directs similarly snide gestures at them, they will resent it deeply.

4. Arrogant leaders tend to interrupt others

Arrogant leaders are often impatient with others and want to share their point of view as quickly as possible; this is because they believe they have the best ideas in the room, and that their contributions outweigh others'. They don't actually care what others are thinking, which is what makes arrogance such a dangerous trait in a leader. Failing to value others' contributions is dangerous, because this limits your perspective and the insights available to you. Ironically, studies have demonstrated that arrogance is correlated with *lower* intelligence scores (Jenks & Steele, 2012) and *lower* self-esteem (Silverman, Johnson, McConnell & Carr, 2012; Johnson, Silverman, Shyamsunder, Swee, Rodopon, Cho & Bauer, 2010). Consider that for a moment: arrogant leaders believe they are smarter than everyone else, but they are not. The problem is that they don't know it.

5. Arrogant leaders talk too much and listen too little

They are often *terrible* listeners. Colleagues recognize this and often stop participating in meetings and discussions, because they know their ideas and perspectives will not be heard. Why waste effort arguing with a leader, if that leader believes they already know everything?

6. Arrogant leaders are unwilling to apologize for inappropriate behaviors

If confronted about behaviors such as yelling at others, putting people down, making mean or sarcastic remarks, or "hogging the show," a truly arrogant leader is unlikely to apologize; they regard an apology as beneath them. They may also feel (or even communicate) that their colleagues deserved the behavior, having earned it through lack of intelligence, ineptitude, or by simply being wrong. So, why apologize? This attitude leaves others with hurt and resentment, and without a sense of closure. It may also leave them with anxiety, because they cannot predict when the hurtful behaviors will occur again. That unpredictability keeps colleagues on edge. Leaders need to understand that apologizing is a courageous and humble act. Unfortunately, arrogant leaders often don't possess an abundance of either courage or humility.

Finally, I have often been struck by the fact that while arrogant leaders may exhibit these behaviors around colleagues, peers, or subordinates, they usually dampen these aggravating and arrogant behaviors around their own supervisors or senior leaders. About 90% of arrogant leaders are able to choose whether or not to display these behaviors. That is hopeful—because if you can actually choose the behavior, you can change it. The remaining 10%, unfortunately, are arrogant with everyone. These individuals lack the discernment and judgment to understand context.

It's important to realize that arrogant leaders will never be able to really lead others. People have to respect and trust you if they are going to follow you. The best that arrogant leaders can hope for is compliance—not commitment.

The Impact of the Arrogant Leader

"It's a stupid way to operate in a complex and changing environment." – Jenks & Steele, 2012.

Jim Collins describes the five predictable stages of failing companies in his excellent book *How the Mighty Fall* (2009). Beginning with the stage of "hubris born of success," he suggests that leadership arrogance lies at the very heart of the path to failure—as organizational leaders become self-congratulatory, convinced of their own importance and brilliance, and closed to contrary ideas, emerging trends, and opportunities for learning.

Jim Collins' "hubris born of success" is a useful lens through which to examine arrogant leadership. Many arrogant leaders are initially quite successful in their careers. They often exhibit a functional or technical expertise that enables them to achieve real results rather quickly. They can prove decisive at times and are often willing to step up to a challenge and take real risk—risks that make others nervous and hesitant (Jenks & Steele, 2012). Often, they are high-energy people, which makes them more noticeable to others. And if they have some charisma to begin with, these individuals begin to "look just like a leader."

There have been leaders who are famously arrogant *and* successful—Steve Jobs, Larry Summers, Henry Kissinger, etc.—but these are as rare as blue diamonds. The vast majority of arrogant leaders produce a very limited positive impact and take far more from their organizations than they ever give.

We have reviewed the "warning behaviors" of arrogant leaders. Now let's review the **5 most frequent impacts** that arrogant leaders have. Let's look at why arrogant leadership is dangerous for a campus:

1. Arrogant leaders foster a "seduction of the leader" dynamic

As described earlier in Chapter 2 of this book, the *seduction of the leader* is a climate in which leaders, especially senior leaders, do not receive honest feedback, opinions, or advice from those they lead, even if they do ask for feedback. Arrogant leaders are especially susceptible to this dynamic, and often actively foster it—leading to situations in which they are left isolated and uninformed. There are several ways in which this dynamic develops around arrogant leaders and creates a cycle of misinformation:

- **People know the leader isn't *really* open to honest feedback** because of the leader's previous reactions to contrary ideas or debate. The leader's reputation precedes them, so colleagues stop offering feedback or ideas. In some cases, they may even be willing to see the arrogant leader fail. They may think, "If that leader knows everything, let *them* fix the mess they are going to create."

  (A question to consider: What is *your* reputation for openness on campus?)

- **There may be a history of penalty for dissent.** Some may have been punished for voicing strong opinions or ideas that are different from the leader's. Punishments may have included public humiliation, disinvitation from important meetings, being cut out of the information loop, or derision toward these individuals' participation and contributions.

- **People may suppress their honest views in order to secure "seats at the table."** In other words, when important decisions are being discussed and made, those wanting to remain part of the process may "go along to get along." They may believe that if they voice their feedback or disagreement too strongly, they will be excluded from the process.

- **In the collegial culture of higher education, individuals may be averse to conflict to begin with.** This can make the task of voicing opinions or feedback to an arrogant leader appear daunting—and even exhausting. Interacting with an arrogant leader can require significant emotional energy and stamina, and people are left having to decide whether their opinion or perspective is worth fighting for.

I have reviewed scores of 360° feedback processes of arrogant leaders, and this theme keeps recurring. People often tell the arrogant leader that if they had only listened to others, they could be very effective. People providing 360° feedback even point out specific examples of failures that could have be avoided *if* the arrogant leader had only listened to others. But arrogant leaders neither seek nor listen to advice, and that is their tragic flaw. Even if the data is clear and powerful, it is often ignored.

2. Arrogant leaders may produce unneeded and wasteful conflict

By succumbing to the "seduction of the leader," arrogant leaders may avoid or suppress *needed* conflict in which their views and perspectives are challenges—but these same leaders often produce a lot of *unneeded* conflict.

One of the many tragic flaws of arrogant leaders is that they cannot always differentiate between the important and the trivial. They see each discussion as a battle to be won and will expend a great deal of energy arguing their point of view to win the day. This is true whether the topic of the discussion is a decision about strategic resource allocation or where the group should go for lunch. Because of the amount of ego that may be involved, the arrogant leader will want their own way in either case.

This can also create an environment in which other leaders on campus simply don't want to back down from such an offensive individual—on anything. If all parties begin to see conversations as win/lose propositions only, then you can arrive at a climate in which a lot of "bar fights" occur between the arrogant leader and peers with the same power on campus. Often, these fights don't occur over topics that are actually strategic or important; they waste leaders' time (Jenks & Steele, 2012) and don't move the campus forward.

Often, institutional stories and legends are created that describe in detail the divisive debates that occur (e.g., "You won't believe what Dr. Johnson said about Dr. Bueller's latest 'silly' proposal" or "Did you hear how bad the marketing meeting was? I am glad I wasn't there!"). Arrogant leaders keep the rumor mill busy by creating negativity on campus, rather than fostering dialogue about what's best for the institution.

3. Arrogant leaders fail to look forward

Arrogant leaders fail to gather the intelligence and perspectives needed to address crises and challenges that affect the institution's future.

As we face the "adaptive" and complex challenges (Heifetz & Linsky, 2002) that are coming at us quickly throughout our campuses, we need leaders who are very open to contrary ideas, different perspectives, opposing views, and creative or even outlandish proposals.

Arrogant leaders can put a campus in peril because they think they know all the answers already. When a campus faces pressing challenges that are complex and ambiguous, arrogant leaders often fail to seek the additional perspectives and ideas needed to overcome that challenge.

What we need in these situations is creative risk taking, experimentation, and the imagination to think outside the box—but if the new idea isn't something the arrogant leader thought up themselves, they may not assign any currency or value to it. These leaders fall into the trap of "listening to themselves too much." They will often take their units or their institutions down the wrong path, remain oblivious to data that contradicts their assumptions and appears predictive of a failing course. They "fly blind," supremely confident in their own abilities and intelligence.

4. Arrogant leaders fail to build a high-performing team

Arrogant leaders can never build a great team (Sanaghan, 2013; Lencioni, 2002; Katzenbach & Smith, 2003; Colvin, 2006). This is a real problem, because the future of our institutions will depend heavily on effective cross-boundary collaboration and on the outstanding work of highly effective teams. Arrogant leadership prevents these teams from forming, for several reasons:

- High-performing teams thrive on honest feedback, debate, and dialogue; on the open sharing of contrary ideas; on curiosity; and on explanation and respect. As we mentioned above, these are not things that arrogant leaders tend to value.

- Arrogant leaders tend to engage in "comfortable cloning," by which team members are chosen and added because they share background, thinking styles, and philosophies that are similar to the leader's. They are unlikely to challenge the leader with new perspectives or insights. In other words, arrogant leaders don't surround themselves with people who will test and stretch their thinking.

- In selecting team members, arrogant leaders often settle for mediocrity rather than striving for excellence. They don't want people on their team who are more talented or intelligent than they are.

So although we need world-class, collaborative teams throughout our campuses as we face the greatest challenges in this generation of higher education, arrogant leaders are ill-equipped to build these teams.

5. Arrogant leaders don't build the relational capital needed in tough times

In higher education, a team or work group doesn't operate in isolation; there are cultural and political boundaries a leader needs to be able to cross in order to gather resources and support for the team. In any initiative worth pursuing, the leader will need the support and help of others throughout the campus; "going alone" will not work.

The leader needs to be prepared and able to ask for help, whether that help consists of advice, personal support, additional strategic thinking, political power, or physical resources. Arrogant leaders tend to be ineffective at boundary management (Hackman, 2002; Sanaghan,

Goldstein, & Trump, 2008), and the problem the arrogant leader faces is twofold. First, they rarely ask for help. Second, by the time they do ask, there is little goodwill left toward them.

The reason for the latter is that people throughout the campus will be reluctant to work with the arrogant leader unless forced to do so. If they are required to do so, they will want to *finish* working with them as quickly as possible. Unfortunately, many of the challenges we face in higher education today are "sticky," complex, and longstanding, so that the arrogant leader often becomes the aggravating and loud neighbor that colleagues in other departments simply have to put up with. That is not a recipe for institutional success.

Ultimately, when the arrogant leader stumbles, colleagues who may be very nice people are nevertheless unmotivated to assist. They may think, "If that leader and their team are so great, as they are always telling us, they should be able to figure this out for themselves." This is a predictable and human response, but it can hurt the overall performance of a department or division.

Exceptional teams recognize that we are always depending on others for assistance in achieving our goals and that cross-boundary collaboration is needed. Those who lead such teams are good at building the relational capital necessary to achieve important things. When that capital is missing, the team's outcomes remain minimal despite their best efforts (Sanaghan, 2013; Hackman, 2002; Lencioni, 2002; Colvin, 2006, 2010). Arrogant leaders and their teams fail to realize this, and they are rarely able to build the relationships and connections needed to achieve stellar performance in the interdependent campus environment.

CASE STUDY: FAILING TO LEARN FROM FAILURES

About a year ago, I received a call from a former client who I had helped in implementing a successful strategic planning process. During the call, she asked me if I was interested in helping with what she described as a "peculiar" challenge. It seems that they wanted to create an integrated "Student First" program to ensure a smooth delivery of student services, and they were on their *third* attempt to do this. Would I be willing to visit the campus and see if I could be helpful? I asked several questions at the start to assess the situation; one of these questions was the "game changer" and appeared to startle my colleague: *"Tell me about the senior leader(s) who has been in charge of the two previous failures, and do they have a role in your third attempt?"*

My colleague communicated that the same senior vice president (SVP) had led the two previous efforts and was handling this third attempt as well, because the project was "his baby." I asked her to describe this SVP for me. She was hesitant with her answers, and used descriptors like: "really, really smart"; "a 'big' personality"; "larger than life"—but not the best listener or team player. A portrait of the SVP began to emerge during our conversation, and it wasn't a positive one. She finally admitted that the SVP was "very arrogant" and even disrespectful to others, and that colleagues had found it difficult to work with him because he already "had all the answers."

Despite two big and expensive failures, this leader had continued to be both arrogant and ineffective. I told my former client that the smartest thing they could do would be to replace the SVP, because there was a very good chance he would fail again—and dramatically.

Unless he was willing to listen to others and reflect on his past practices so he could learn from what hadn't worked, I would not be interested in helping out. She asked me if I would be willing to at least have a phone meeting with him. Given our positive past history, I reluctantly agreed.

I put a call in to him and we had a very brief conversation. I asked him what he had learned from the past two attempts at implementing the Student First initiative. He was not happy with the question. "Pat," he said, "I don't need to look back. I only move forward as a leader. That's just the way I lead, and I expect others to follow me. That's what real leaders do."

I pushed back on the answer. (I wasn't one of his peers or subordinates; I could afford to push back.) "I have found that reflecting back on what worked and didn't work just makes you smarter in going forward. I would also hope that you would be interested in learning about how effective your leadership was with the two previous attempts."

He wasn't interested. I wished him good luck, and the conversation ended abruptly.

Unfortunately, that SVP continues to stumble forward, ignoring any evidence that he may need to change his approach—and wasting colleagues' time and the institution's funds in the process. The president is aware of the situation and will likely have to step in either to relieve him of his duty or to insist that he seek expert coaching and listen and learn from it. Colleagues on campus are busy betting which way it will go. The odds don't look very good for the SVP.

Comparing Arrogant Leaders with Effective Leaders

In the recent study *Decoding Leadership: What Really Matters* (2015), researchers identified a set of 20 leadership traits that correlated to leadership success. They further honed the list by surveying 189,000 people in 81 diverse organizations around the world, identifying four critical leadership behaviors that explained 80% of the variance between strong and weak organizations in terms of leadership effectiveness.

These four behaviors were:

1. Being supportive of their people.

2. Operating with a strong results orientation.

3. Seeking different perspectives.

4. Solving problems effectively.

Conversely, the research on arrogance tells us that arrogant leaders are *not* supportive of their people, often take credit for their work, and do not develop junior staff (Jenks & Steele, 2012, McLean & Elkind, 2013; Silverman, Johnson, McConnell & Carr, 2012; Irwin, 2012). And because arrogant leaders fail to seek different perspectives (because they already know it all) and are terrible listeners when different perspectives are offered, they are prevented from solving problems effectively.

When we look at those four behaviors of effective leaders, arrogant leaders score low in three out of the four. How then can they be effective in their role?

Strategies to Adopt When Faced with an Arrogant Leader

Given everything this chapter has discussed, is there hope for the arrogant leaders? Yes, there is. But it is a long shot. Let's look at another case study.

CASE STUDY: THE ARROGANT CFO

About a decade ago I was asked to work with a Chief Business Officer who was well-accomplished but arrogant in his leadership style. He transitioned into a campus with a messy and confusing financial situation that lacked established financial protocols and procedures. The CBO—we'll call him "Chuck"—came in and "cleaned things up" in a relatively short period of time. The president deeply valued both his technical skills and his strong work ethic.

Unfortunately, Chuck was not a team player, and members of the senior team found working with him disagreeable, distasteful, and difficult. He talked too much in team meetings, boasted about his accomplishments, took credit for his subordinates' good work, and talked over his colleagues. The other leaders on campus avoided working with him on campus projects, because Chuck always "had all the answers" to complex challenges and belittled others' ideas. Everyone gave him credit for dramatically improving the financial situation and admired how hard he worked—but they hated working with him.

The president was concerned that Chuck's negative impact on team members would impair the senior team's effectiveness in a challenging and competitive environment. Something had to be done with Chuck, but the president didn't want to lose him.

After interviewing everyone on the senior team, including Chuck, I suggested that the entire team conduct a Leadership Audit (Sanaghan & Lohndorf, 2015), which is an informal, qualitative assessment process that provides participants with powerful and anonymous feedback about their effectiveness as leaders. The audit, in its simplest form, consists of three simple questions (for a more involved look at a Leadership Audit, see pages 71-74):

1. What are my five greatest strengths as a leader?

2. What is one area of needed development I should be aware of and conscious about?

3. What is one piece of advice you would like to provide me that would help me in my current role?

Not surprisingly, Chuck had never previously received anonymous feedback about his leadership style. Although he knew he could be considered "overbearing," he had little idea about the pervasiveness of the impact he had on the senior team.

He received lots of positive feedback that was well deserved (e.g., bright, hardworking, and strong technical skills). He also received strong feedback on ways to develop and grow as a leader (e.g., you need to listen to people; you are very difficult to work with; people don't want to share information with you because of your judgmental and harsh criticism; and you interrupt people too much).

He was stunned by the "constructive" feedback he received—and hurt that people found working with him to be uncomfortable. He and I spent several hours discussing the implications and the feedback and what he might think about changing. We agreed to meet several days later and develop an action plan that would help him change the negative behaviors and people's perceptions of his effectiveness.

Initially, based on my past experience in working with arrogant leaders, I was not very hopeful about his commitment to work on his arrogant behavior.

I was wrong.

To his great credit, Chuck took the information gleaned from the Leadership Audit and was committed to working on neutralizing his negative impact. We connected him with a local executive coach who was deeply experienced and was used to working with "strong personalities." Chuck's action plan focused on changing three specific behaviors over the course of a year. He and his coach took one at a time, worked on it, and then moved to the next one. They did not attempt to work on all three at the same time.

The plan looked like this:

A) Chuck dedicated himself to watching how he interacted in meetings, especially how often he interrupted others. He kept a quiet count of his interruptions during his weekly meetings with his team. Over several months, he improved dramatically. As a result, he saw more participation from members of his team. He also gained a deeper trust in the intelligence of his people and their desire to contribute.

B) Chuck learned to count to seven silently before responding to others in a group meeting, especially if there was a strong difference of opinion. This allowed him time to gather his thoughts before responding too quickly. It also communicated that he was actually willing to listen to others, which almost always conveys respect.

C) Lastly, he really worked on developing his active listening skills. He would reflect back what he was hearing from others, especially when he disagreed with them. This was not easy, and it took discipline and practice.

These three small yet important behaviors changed how he interacted with people and how he was perceived. At first, there was some real doubt from his colleagues about his authenticity with this changed behavior—but he persisted over time and won many people over. We conducted an informal assessment in a 6-month and 12-month review, and his colleagues reported that they saw real changes in his leadership and found working with him more tolerable. The working relationship hadn't become pleasant overnight, but it was no longer *un*pleasant and ineffective.

What Chuck's example reveals is that, in many cases, an arrogant leader *can* be made aware of their impact—and that there are specific strategies for mitigating that impact and for helping them change course. In this section of the chapter, we will review these strategies from several perspectives:

1. Strategies to use if you supervise an arrogant leader.

2.   Strategies to use if your peer is an arrogant leader.

3.   Strategies to use if you report to an arrogant leader.

4.   An informal self-assessment audit (and advice) to determine and respond if *you* are, at least to some degree, an arrogant leader.

Strategies to Use if You Supervise an Arrogant Leader

"Curtail arrogance early in a leader's career." – Silverman, et al, 2012.

The above quote is the best advice we can give when dealing with arrogant leaders. You need to nip arrogant behavior "in the bud" as quickly as possible. Arrogance grows like a weed and will poison a team, work group, or task force quickly. We simply cannot afford the toxic impact of arrogant leaders on our campuses. No matter what results they *might* achieve, the price you will pay for those results is never worth it.

The good news is that, almost always, arrogant behavior is quite visible. Identifying the problem is the easy part.

You may recognize some of the following strategies from the earlier chapters on *seduction of the leader* and the *derailment of the leader*—because arrogant leaders are especially susceptible to the "seduction" dynamic and are especially likely to derail. None of the following ideas are guaranteed to work, but all of them have worked some of the time. It will take persistence, patience, and perspiration to manage an arrogant leader well. All we can ever really do is provide feedback, choices, support, and vigilant attention to the situation. In the end, the arrogant leader must choose their path forward, and only those with courage, emotional intelligence, and integrity are likely to make the journey.

A note of caution:

- If you are dealing with a younger, emerging leader, the chances of improving their leadership skillset and neutralizing their arrogant behaviors are quite good.

- Unfortunately, working with a more "mature" leader, say 50+ years old, who has been arrogant for decades, is a different and difficult challenge. It is a long shot but not impossible. When I met Chuck, in our case study, he was about 50 years old. Shifting course was a challenging journey for him, but he was committed to improving his leadership. Often, it takes an "opportunity" or a "crisis" to prompt real change.

Here are some steps to take if you supervise an arrogant leader.

1. Engage in a 360° Feedback Process

Undertaking this dynamic and powerful learning process, in which leaders receive anonymous and honest feedback from their colleagues, is a courageous act for any leader but is *especially* so for arrogant ones. You can read a description of the process on pages 23-24.

For many arrogant leaders, the 360° provides a dose of surprising, harsh, and tough information. It creates a *choice point* for the leader. Although they might not choose to change their behavior even after they learn how people perceive them, they will clearly understand their negative impact on others. That's the only thing you can provide—the *opportunity* to learn and grow. You can't force someone to be less arrogant; they have to decide that for themselves.

If an arrogant leader undertakes a 360° feedback process, they need to be aware that people will now know that they have received information about their strengths and weaknesses, and people will *expect a change in their behavior*. If change doesn't happen, the leader will lose credibility fast and will be unable to really lead others.

2. Get an Executive Coach

Executive coaching for an arrogant leader can be a helpful approach—but will only be effective if the leader is genuinely interested in changing their behavior. Many will not be. Note that coaching focuses on behavior, not on trying to change the arrogant person's mind. Coaching is also not the same as therapy; it isn't intended to determine the reason the arrogance is there (Weinstock & Sanaghan, 2015).

If the leader is motivated to seek an executive coach (often at risk of demotion, termination, or visibly on the road to derailing), the coach might work with the leader on practices like:

Learning not to interrupt

Quantity of interruptions can be monitored over time, and they can seek feedback from those they work with.

Counting to seven

In our case study, Chuck began counting to seven silently before responding to others in a group discussion or team meeting. This is an important practice because arrogant leaders are often whiplash quick in conversations. They may finish people's sentences or cut them off mid-sentence. They are interested in "moving things along," so they can hurry to voice *their* ideas. Slowing down the response can allow other members of the team to participate and can open the possibility of providing the arrogant leader with new information. (Possibly.)

Committing to arrive at meetings on time

It is important that arrogant leaders convey respect for others' time. And, if they are late, they need to apologize quickly for their lateness.

Practicing active listening

This takes practice and patience, but it can be a game changer. It is one of the behaviors that an executive coach can help a leader develop and practice.

What all these practices have in common is that they are intended to remove obstacles to the leader receiving new information. This is critical. Limited information and limited receptivity to information is one of the major reasons that arrogant leaders derail.

I recall one senior vice president who, after initial success, saw their strategic initiative fail in a highly visible way. The president of the institution ordered an After Action Review (AAR) to determine what had gone wrong. I conducted the review process with several other key leaders who had also been involved in the debacle, and I made sure that the arrogant leader was not present for the debrief. He was not happy with that decision, but it permitted the safety for the debrief to surface one pervasive theme—that if the arrogant leader had just listened to people, he would have seen that all the information needed to avert the disaster was available. But the leader had not been open to others' opinions and had regularly shut down debate.

When this information was shared with the arrogant leader, he was stunned and vowed to change his behavior. He took several courses in active listening and connected with an executive coach. Over time, he became a good (though not a great) listener. In his case, he was highly motivated—he didn't want to fail a second time in the full view of everyone.

CONNECT WITH THE BEST EXECUTIVE COACHES

Executive Coaching with Academic Impressions can help leaders gain clarity in their career and reach their full potential. You can learn more about Executive Coaching at:

https://www.academicimpressions.com/execu tive-coaching/

3. Commit to an Effective Supervisory Process

Effective supervision is one of the best ways to manage an arrogant leader's behavior (Sanaghan & Lohndorf, 2015). The supervisory process should have clear goals and objectives that are negotiated and understood by the arrogant leader up front. Appropriate support is also crucial if the supervision is to create the context for success. Support might include quality time with the boss, enough resources to do the job, managing the workload so that it doesn't become overwhelming, and frequent check-ins and conversations.

The key to an effective supervisory process is *consistent feedback* about the arrogant leader's behavior and effectiveness. This should include what their supervisor observes, as well as *anonymous* peer feedback. The anonymous feedback is an essential element of the process. The arrogant leader needs to understand deeply the negative impact of their behavior on others and on the team's performance.

That feedback should also be balanced with feedback affirming some of the positive contributions the leader makes (e.g., getting things done, their work ethic, or their ability to push ideas forward). The goal here is not to "beat the person up," but to show them a rich and more complete picture of themselves, to provide opportunity for them to gain insight and make different choices.

This rigorous feedback process should be conducted on a quarterly basis, *not* just once a year. This will obviously take time and attention on the part of the supervisor, but it is an effective practice to implement. This consistent and frequent feedback will provide the arrogant leader with critical information that hopefully will encourage them to neutralize their negative impact and increase their positive contributions.

Having specific behaviors to work on (e.g., not interrupting others; soliciting people's ideas; not being sarcastic) is important, because these will act as behavioral markers for the leader. They need to clearly understand *what* they are working on improving. This might sound obvious, but identifying and monitoring specific behaviors is a critical element in the supervisory process.

With their help of their supervisor, some arrogant leaders may begin to change their behavior and (hopefully) receive more positive feedback from others as they continue on their learning journey.

For more information about an effective supervisory dialogue, see the Appendix at the end of this book.

4. Seek Anonymous Feedback with a "Leadership Audit"

You can find a description of the Leadership Audit on pages 71-74 of this book. It is a powerful but simple tool for collecting quick, anonymous feedback for the leader.

Two notes of caution about the use of a Leadership Audit in a case in which there is an arrogant leader:

First, this might be the first time that an arrogant leader receives anonymous and honest information about their behaviors. Although the Leadership Audit focuses on *both* strengths and areas of needed development, some leaders will learn for the first time how people actually experience them. For many, this can be quite shocking. There may even be some "cutting" comments. Someone might write "Quit being a know-it-all; it isn't helpful," or "Your sarcasm is a huge turnoff and really angers people," or "Who do you think you are, interrupting everyone all the time?" Taking the Leadership Audit is not a journey for the faint of heart. The good news is that the leader will also hear objective takes on the strengths they bring to the table.

This is where good supervision is essential. The supervisor must dedicate the time to listen to the arrogant leader's reactions and responses to the data they receive—and must help them makes sense of it. There might be a need to provide further support from the human resources department. The bottom line is that this support is critical to the leader's learning journey—even if the arrogant leader doesn't ask for it.

Second, never create a situation where only a single leader is taking the Leadership Audit. This will send a signal to others that there might be a problem or that the arrogant leader is "in trouble." Often, this will encourage people to really pile it on and "tell it like it is." This will defeat the intent of the Audit, because the Audit is not designed to be a vehicle for punishment but a learning process.

At a minimum, the supervisor should also agree to engage in the Leadership Audit, along with the arrogant leader they supervise. Even better, engage the entire team in the Audit process so they can take a shared risk together, learn about their leadership impact, and provide constructive feedback to each other.

Strategies to Use if Your Peer is an Arrogant Leader

There are strategies you can use if you and the arrogant leader have equal status. It's more difficult, after all, to "roll over" a peer. Also, the arrogant leader might actually need your help, and providing that help can create more balance in the relationship.

It is important to note that the following strategies have worked well with many arrogant leaders, but *only* if you are a peer. These strategies will not be successful if you occupy a subordinate position to the person in question.

If you are a peer, though, here are some things to try:

1. Create Working "Ground Rules"

If you have an ongoing relationship with an arrogant peer, you can suggest strongly that you agree on some ground rules for your interactions and discussions with each other.

For example, you might suggest: "You and I will need to work together collaboratively and effectively on this project, and I want both of us to be successful. I also want to be the best working partner I can be for you. I want to suggest that we agree on three ground rules for working together:

- "We will not interrupt each other during discussions.

- "We will use active listening when we disagree so that the other person at least feels heard & understood.

- "As much as possible, we will use facts, data, and information to inform the important decisions we will need to make together."

This might seem simple, but it can be a game changer. If you can hold each other accountable to a *small* set of ground rules, you can keep the interactions tolerable— maybe not enjoyable, but workable.

2. Create Specific Criteria When Making Important Decisions

Arrogant people push their opinions and perspectives hard, convinced that they are right. Often, facts do not persuade or dissuade them, because they value their own experience and their assumptions more; they "just know what the right course of action is."

If you are part of a team or work group, it is very helpful for the members to generally agree on a handful of rigorous criteria for a good decision *before* you get into the debate and discussion. You should reserve the creation of such criteria for important decisions—those decisions where getting it right really matters, such as when you are deciding to undertake a new strategic initiative. These criteria can provide the necessary structure and guidance for making an effective decision vs. "winging it."

For example, when deciding among a range of strategic initiatives, you might establish criteria like the following to select the best initiative:

- **It must play to our strength as an institution.** (That is: we know how to do it, we have experience with it; we have done something similar before. It can't be something totally new to us.)

- **It must be able to enhance the reputation and the brand**. (It must be visible to others and make a difference in the community.)

- **It has to use existing technology.** (We can't afford to invest a lot of new money with expensive and sophisticated technology.)

- **It must be aligned with our strategic plan.** (It needs to add value to our existing goals and objectives and not create a misdirection.)

- **It has to be something we can begin to implement within 30 days.** (We don't want to spend a year planning and get bogged down in process.)

Spending time developing the criteria will almost always create some discipline in the decision making process, because at the end of the day, the best initiative must meet the *agreed upon criteria*, versus one arrogant person's forceful ideas.

3. Elevate the Discussion If You Can

One of the themes we have discussed in this chapter is that the arrogant leader confuses the important with the trivial. If you are caught in a debate with an arrogant leader, consider "elevating" the conversation by referring to the campus' mission, values, and vision. These can provide an honorable framework for conversation. If your campus values *inclusivity*, you can mention that "by not shutting down debate and involving more people in the discussion, you mirror our stated values as an institution." Other institutional values like *respect* should always be a part of our discussions and debates. Another example: "The *spirit of inquiry* matters in higher education and to our rich history, and can be invoked in defending the need to explore multiple perspectives before we make important decisions about the future."

4. Seek Advice from Those Who Know Them Best

This is a technique that I have seen work several times with "difficult" leaders. Find out who their professional friends are (hopefully, they have some) and ask them for some "advice" on how to work with the arrogant leader.

For example, you might approach such a professional friend as follows: "Mary, I know that you get along with Pierre pretty well. I also know that he is smart, and we can learn some great things from him, but I find him 'difficult' to work with at times. He doesn't seem to listen well and he can roll over people in meetings. Do you have any advice or insight that might be helpful to me? I want to make this relationship to work."

Two positive things might happen. First, Mary might be able to provide some real, practical advice that can help you navigate conversations with your arrogant peer.

The second thing that *might* happen is that Mary may connect informally with Pierre and discuss the conversation she had with you and the advice she gave. Pierre *might* be surprised to learn about his impact with others and might actually listen to feedback—or seek you out to better understand his behavior. It's a long shot, but I have seen it work.

Strategies to Use if You Report to an Arrogant Leader

If you are a subordinate to an arrogant leader, this is a very difficult situation, especially because:

- Arrogant leaders often deal harshly with those who disagree with them.

- They prevent others from presenting a contrary point of view. ("If I already know the answer," the arrogant leader may think, "why muddy the waters with other people's nonsense?")

- They act condescendingly towards subordinates. This can be appalling to witness at times. At best, they are unaware of the impact of their behavior on others. At worst, they don't care.

- They get angry quickly when subordinates don't "get" the merit of their perspective or their ideas.

- They often put subordinates who challenge their ideas "in their place" in no uncertain terms. ("If you only knew more about this situation," an arrogant leader might say, "you wouldn't make *that* suggestion, *ever.*")

This doesn't mean the situation is hopeless—just very difficult. The following suggestions *might* help a subordinate when dealing with an arrogant leader:

1. Never take on an arrogant superior directly

This is a "fool's game." They will take deep offense and will likely penalize you. Arrogant leaders can engage in retaliatory behavior when they are angry, so you need to be careful.

2. Try not to take their arrogance personally.

It's not about you; it's about them. Arrogant leaders act inappropriately because of low self-esteem and a need to insist on their importance. It's difficult but important to remember that their behaviors are not a response to you personally.

3. If you find yourself in debate with an arrogant leader, use facts as much as possible.

In some cases, an arrogant leader can be persuaded by facts to take a second look—though this is not a given. You need to present facts carefully, because arrogant leaders may respond with anger if they feel you are "trying to outsmart" them.

4. Pick your battles carefully.

Make sure the topic or subject is really important to you, so that challenging an arrogant leader's perspective is worth the aggravation and the risk. If you do determine that this is a necessary discussion to hold or a necessary battle to fight, avoid any confrontational tone or language. Be firm and calm.

5. Find ways to "elevate" the discussion.

Refer to the institution's values and mission, and to the higher goals your efforts serve. It's important to take the conversation to a different level and not cast it solely as a debate between strong opinions

6. Find ways to be helpful.

An arrogant leader likes to "look good"—if you can help them "look good" to others, you can build a connection with them. In turn, if they know that you are helpful to them, they may approach you with less of an "edge."

7. Take care of yourself.

Lastly, do whatever you can to relieve your stress. Take a walk to center yourself before meeting with the arrogant leader. Meditate. Use journaling to capture your thoughts and feelings. "Treat" yourself after an unpleasant confrontation. Find whatever stress relievers work for you, and take care to yourself.

Are *You* an Arrogant Leader?

The following informal assessment includes a set of questions that have been sourced from the research on arrogance: Jenks & Steele (2012); Silverman, et al (2010); Johnson, et al (2010).

If you have the courage to answer these questions honestly, they will give you an informative snapshot of your current level of personal and professional arrogance.

Other uses of this assessment

Some people have used this as an informal assessment for problem employees they supervise. Using *observed* behavior, you can imagine how your "problem" employee will answer these questions. This can provide some insight into their level of arrogance. It may also be helpful to ask them to score themselves *after* you have scored them. This way you can compare and contrast your answers and get a conversation going. That conversation is critical, however difficult, because simply ignoring arrogant behavior is not a strategy for mitigating its impact.

Obviously, this is *not* without risk but it might be helpful in creating a meaningful conversation. You owe it to your employee to give them an honest assessment of your perspective and share it with them. If you both find that the arrogance level is rather high, you can then discuss some of the implications and impacts and, most importantly, use some of the strategies in this chapter to hopefully change the arrogant behavior—or at least neutralizing its impact. Remember to use specific examples (e.g., interrupting others, using sarcasm in team meetings, acting impatient, rolling eyes, etc.) when you discuss the person's arrogance. They often don't see their arrogance or their negative impact on others, so the examples are important and might create a choice point for them.

Please pay careful attention to how the statements are phrased.

An Informal Arrogance Self-Assessment

1. The quality of thinking of the people I work with often frustrates me.

1	2	3	4	5
Strongly Disagree	Disagree	Neutral	Agree	Strongly Agree

2. I am rarely uncertain about my ideas and opinions.

1	2	3	4	5
Strongly Disagree	Disagree	Neutral	Agree	Strongly Agree

3. I really don't appreciate it when people I work with push back on my ideas and proposals.

1	2	3	4	5
Strongly Disagree	Disagree	Neutral	Agree	Strongly Agree

4. Being a "team player" is highly overrated.

1	2	3	4	5
Strongly Disagree	Disagree	Neutral	Agree	Strongly Agree

5. If I am honest with myself, I am not really curious about what other people think.

1	2	3	4	5
Strongly Disagree	Disagree	Neutral	Agree	Strongly Agree

6. I know who I am, and soliciting feedback from others about my effectiveness would be a waste of time.

1	2	3	4	5
Strongly Disagree	Disagree	Neutral	Agree	Strongly Agree

7. I truly believe that if I left this place on short notice, things would fall apart quickly.

1	2	3	4	5
Strongly Disagree	Disagree	Neutral	Agree	Strongly Agree

8. I really don't think there is any challenge too daunting for me.

1	2	3	4	5
Strongly Disagree	Disagree	Neutral	Agree	Strongly Agree

9. I often find myself feeling impatient with others, because I have to wait until they catch up to my thinking and ideas.

1	2	3	4	5
Strongly Disagree	Disagree	Neutral	Agree	Strongly Agree

10. I am _not_ very good at listening to others.

1	2	3	4	5
Strongly Disagree	Disagree	Neutral	Agree	Strongly Agree

How to score the survey

Please add up the scores you have given for the ten statements. For example, you might end up with 36 total points. Then divide that total by 10 (the number of statements), and you will get your "average" score. In this example, it would be 3.6.

To interpret the results:

A score *below a 2* is a great score for *not* being arrogant.

If you find yourself giving the "neutral" number 3 a lot, there are a few things to think about:

- A "3" is what we call a "timid" score. You weren't sure—but when we have probed people about their answers, they tend to migrate toward a "4."

- Some individuals say a 3 or a "neutral" score is a "silent no," and you may be unsure about your arrogance "quotient." If this is the case, review your scores again and really try to respond to each question with either a 2 or a 4; stay away from too many 3's.

A score of *3* is an indication of arrogance. In this case, you will want to watch your behavior carefully, because it can easily migrate to a strong arrogance score, and you want to avoid this "migration" at all costs. Review some of the behaviors we highlighted in the first section of this chapter and try to eliminate one of those behaviors – not all of them at once. Become more conscious of *one* behavior (e.g., derision, being late to meetings, interrupting people, or showing impatience) and focus on neutralizing it. That will be doable and will make a significant difference in your work place, with your interactions with others, and on your overall impact.

A score of _4_ or greater should be a big warning sign. It is probable that people don't like interacting with you and that they put a great deal of effort into avoiding you. This is not an effective place to lead from. If you score a _4_, you have an important choice before you. You have to ask: How much do you care? Are you okay with leading in an arrogant manner? If the answer is _yes_, then attempts to improve may waste your time—and others'. Shifting arrogant behaviors will require courage, discipline, and humility. I highly recommend a 360° feedback process— for _all_ leaders—because then you have an accurate picture of how you are seen by others.

Ways to improve

If your arrogant behaviors have been called out by your team, your supervisors, and/or your peers, or if you have been alerted to arrogant tendencies by the informal self-assessment above, here is some practical advice for moving forward:

Commit to Learning Something New

Many hard-working leaders have strong technical and functional skills that move them up the career leader quickly. They get things done, achieve results, and are often willing to take risks that others shy away from (Jenks & Steele, 2012). Unfortunately, this early career progress can fuel the notion that they are smart _at everything_.

Learning something meaningful and new outside their circle of competence puts them in a _learner's role_. As a "student" learning something new, they can't have all the answers _yet_. They will need to ask for help and guidance, which can be humbling for them and difficult to do, but it can help broaden their portfolio and build their capacity.

Learn to Share Your Thinking With Others

Arrogant leaders rarely explain the rationale behind their "answers" – they just share the answers. It is almost always helpful for *any* leader to explain *how* they came to a particular conclusion or way of thinking (Sanaghan, 2013). This doesn't need to be complex or overly verbal. The following three statements can create a constructive framework for sharing a leader's thinking *and* learning from others. Although this will be counterintuitive for arrogant leaders, I have seen this work effectively several times over the years:

1. "This is my *best current thinking.*" ("Best current" conveys that the leader has *not* yet reached a conclusion).

2. "This is *how* I got to this place/decision point." (The leader can share the information, interviews, research, or their own experiences that have informed their best current thinking.)

3. "Now, please help me understand what I *might* be missing." (This will be difficult for arrogant leaders to ask, but If they solicit the perspective and advice of others actively and sincerely, people will begin to share their ideas, and the leader will be much better informed.)

This simple protocol will feel awkward at first, but if the arrogant leader persists, it will reap many benefits. They will no longer communicate the idea that they know everything; they will convey respect for the ideas of others; they will create some real rigor with their own thinking because they have to show how they got to the decision point; and they will develop better listening skills.

Let Go of the Small Stuff

One of the biggest flaws of arrogant leaders is that they have a hard time separating or discerning the difference between the small and the important things in life. If an arrogant leader perceives their ego as always being on the line, everything can be up for debate. They don't like to back down from an argument and will push hard on even trivial matters. If you have some arrogant tendencies, it can be helpful to identify a handful of really important things you are willing to fight for, and commit to fight hard only on those things. This keeps you from wasting your own time—and others'—and ensures that you are focusing on the strategic items that will help you receive the recognition you seek and deserve.

Remaining mired in the details is counterproductive not only because it wastes time but because it communicates to peers and supervisors that you aren't ready for the next level, where things are even more complicated. Identify the big issues that matter and engage in meaningful dialogue and debate about those.

Summary

It is important to identify and mitigate arrogant leadership early because there is little upside to this leadership style. Arrogant leaders don't build the capacity of their people. They often "fly blind" because they don't listen to or value others' ideas or experience. They often set projects up for failure by neglecting to conduct a rigorous environmental scan or feasibility assessment, and they are ineffective at building collaborative and high-performing teams.

If you supervise leaders with arrogant tendencies, provide them with opportunities to receive anonymous feedback, support them with good supervision and coaching, and hold them accountable to a higher standard. And—this is important—don't fall into the trap of overlooking arrogant behaviors. There is never a time when treating people disrespectfully is acceptable, and overlooking that in the short term creates more trouble in the long term.

References

Collins, James C. *How the Mighty Fall: And Why Some Companies Never Give In.* Random House, 2009.

Colvin, Geoffrey. "What It Takes to Be Great." *Fortune Magazine*, vol. *154*, no. 9, 2006.

—. *Talent Is Overrated.* Penguin Books, 2008.

Dotlich, David L., et al. *Why CEOs Fail: The 11 Behaviors That Can Derail Your Climb to the Top--and How to Manage Them.* John Wiley & Sons, 2003.

Feser, Claudio, et al. "Decoding Leadership: What Really Matters." *McKinsey Quarterly*, February 2015. Retrieved from: http://www.mckinsey.com/global-themes/leadership/decoding-leadership-what-really-matters

Hackman, J. Richard. *Leading Teams: Setting the Stage for Great Performances.* Harvard Business Press, 2002.

Hansen, Morten. *Collaboration: How Leaders Avoid the Traps, Build Common Ground, and Reap Big Results.* Harvard Business Press, 2013.

Hayward, Mathew. *Ego Check: Why Executive Hubris Is Wrecking Companies and Careers and How to Avoid the Trap.* Kaplan Publishing, 2007.

Heifetz, Ronald, et al. *Leadership on the Line: Staying Alive Through the Dangers of Leading.* Harvard Business Press, 2002.

——. *The Practice of Adaptive Leadership.* Harvard Business Review Press, 2009.

Irwin, Tim. *Derailed: Five Lessons Learned from Catastrophic Failures of Leadership.* Thomas Nelson Inc., 2012.

Jenks, Stephen, and Fritz Steele. *The Arrogant Leader: Dealing with Excesses of Power.* National Book Network, 2012.

Johnson, R. E., et al. "Acting Superior but Actually Inferior? Correlates and Consequences of Workplace Arrogance." *Human Performance*, vol. 23, no. 5, 2010, pp. 403-427.

Karlgaard, Rich, and Michael Malone. *Team Genius.* Harper Collins, 2015.

Katzenbach, Jon, and Douglas Smith. *The Wisdom of Teams: Creating the High Performance Organization.* Harper Collins, 2003.

Lencioni, Patrick. *The Five Dysfunctions of a Team: A Leadership Fable.* Jossey-Bass, 2002.

McLean, Bethany, and Peter Elkind. *The Smartest Guys in the Room: The Amazing Rise and Scandalous Fall of Enron.* Penguin, 2013.

Sanaghan, Patrick. "Bad Advice." *Inside Higher Ed,* April 2011. Retrieved from:

https://www.insidehighered.com/advice/2011/04/27/e ssay_on_dangers_faced_by_presidents_who_don_t_get _good_advice

Sanaghan, Patrick, and J. Lohndorf. *Collaborative Leadership: The New Leadership Stance*. Academic Impressions, 2015.

—. *The Derailment of the Leader in Higher Education*. Academic Impressions, February 2015.

Sanaghan, Patrick, et al. *The Exceptional Team Survey*. Human Resources Development Press, 2008.

Silverman, Stanley, et al. "Arrogance: A Formula for Leadership Failure." *The Industrial-Organizational Psychologist*, vol. 50, no. 1, 2012, pp. 21-28.

Stark, Peter, and Mary Kelly. *Why Leaders Fail and the 7 Prescriptions for Success*. Bentley Press, 2016.

Webb, A., Moderator. "When to Change How You Lead." *McKinsey & Company Quarterly*, 2015.

Weinstock, Beth, and Patrick Sanaghan. *Preparing Tomorrow's Leaders: Leadership Coaching in Higher Education*. Academic Impressions, 2015. Retrieved from: https://www.academicimpressions.com/preparing tomorrows-leaders-leadership-coaching-in-higher education/

APPENDIX: SUPERVISORY DIALOGUE

Overview

The "Supervisory Dialogue" was informed and influenced by the initial thinking of Dr. Rodney Napier, a mentor and colleague, over 25 years ago.

Note that the following ideas and proposed process do not deal with some of the legal issues that a supervision process might also include (e.g., bullying, sexual harassment, etc.). It also does not deal with the supervision of grossly ineffective or really poor performing employees. There are plenty of articles and books in the field that deal with these topics.

This supervision process works well with the 95% of employees who work hard everyday and strive to live the mission of their campus. It is focused on the strengths of the employee and helps establish mutual accountability for an employee's success.

It is hoped that this chapter might create real discussion about supervision within your organization and on your campus. In the end, you need to design a supervisory process that meets your unique organizational culture, strategy, values, and goals. This is a suggested process that can be adapted to meet your needs; it has been used successfully in the corporate sector, government, the non-profit sector, and in higher education.

This proposed process works best on the administrative side of the house—we have seen it used effectively by provosts with their deans and by presidents with their cabinets. Given the unique role of the faculty at institutions of higher education, and the context of faculty life, "supervision" is not a word that is used very often with faculty. We believe that this is a missed opportunity, especially for junior faculty, but the unique culture and processes of faculty evaluation and oversight are an institutional reality we must consider with care when thinking about using the Supervisory Dialogue within academic departments.

Some Thoughts

1. Supervision, if it is to be effective, must be valued by the organization. This means that leaders need to be trained, supported, and rewarded for supervision to be truly effective, especially at the top levels of senior management. (This is rarely the case.)

2. Effective supervision communicates to people throughout the organization that investing time and support in people is an *organizational value*. It also communicates that honest feedback, rigorous goal setting, good communication, and developing people is prized by the organization.

3. Supervision is essentially about the relationship between the supervisor and employee. Without an

honest, open, and supportive relationship based on trust, real supervision cannot take place.

The classic Failure of Management by Objectives (M.B.O.) in the 1970's and 80's was due to the lack of attention paid to the relationship between the boss and the subordinate. In theory, it looked great on paper. The boss and subordinate would set mutual goals and performance standards, and everything would be wonderful. Unfortunately, when there is little trust in the organization or between the supervisor and supervisee, employees will set minimal goals. Without trust, people tend not to take risks, stretch themselves, experiment, or make themselves vulnerable. What ends up happening is a negotiation around minimal goals and expectations. In the end, organizations achieve mediocrity.

Pay attention to the relationship; it is the key to effective performance and supervision.

4. The employee is in a vulnerable position in a supervisory process. The supervisor is in the "power" position because he/she can reward or punish the employee. The supervisor needs to be proactive in establishing a safe and trusting relationship with the employee. They can do this by: listening carefully (very difficult to do); providing clear examples of performance; focusing on the strengths of the individual; giving honest feedback; and being interested in the development of the employee.

Unfortunately, supervision is not a sexy topic. The current rage is "leadership." But all the leadership in the world does not produce results. People do. Effective leaders deeply understand that you achieve meaningful results (add value) through the hard work and thinking of people. Supervision enables leaders to accomplish things because it builds the capacity of people, supports their development, and holds them appropriately accountable. It is important but not glitzy work. It is desperately needed in our organizations.

5. Effective supervision takes time. The research shows that we spend an average of an hour a year in some kind of supervisory process with most employees. These tend to be perfunctory sessions, utilizing checklists, and focusing on a one-way dialogue from the supervisor to the supervisee. Real supervision is an investment of time in the employee, but not much time. Somehow we have convinced ourselves that there is no time to do real supervision, because there is too much work to do! We often spend much of our time putting out fires, being reactive, and going from one crisis to another. Too often, people are rewarded for being busy and not for being productive. We often hear leaders say, "I don't have enough time to supervise!" That is a terrible myth.

RESOURCE: "BEWARE THE BUSY MANAGER"

We would suggest that those leaders who are stressed out, hurry all over the place, and feel overwhelmed all the time read a great article, "Beware the Busy Manager" by Heike Bruch and Sumantra Ghoshal, HBR (2002). It is an excellent article that helps the reader understand *why* they are "too busy" and provides some strategies to be more mindful and focused.

The Facts

1. A "typical" workweek is 40 hours (for most of us, it's 50-60 hours).

2. A work year consists of 2000 hours, excluding two weeks for vacation (again, most of us have real work years consisting of 2500-3000 hours per year).

3. The proposed supervisory process/schedule would take approximately 8-10 hours per employee, per year. Which is about 1/2 of 1% of your total available work time. Even if you have 8-10 direct reports, this would take approximately 5% of your work time, leaving you lots of time to do other "important" stuff.

Bottom line: There is no excuse for not investing a fraction of your time in developing your people. If you cannot find the time, look at the results you are producing, not all the busy activity. Too many leaders fall into the "buckets of sweat" syndrome, where there is a whole lot of busy activity but little meaningful production.

The Supervisory Dialogue creates the opportunity to focus on results and performance, and not just the busy work we too often get caught up with.

A Proposed Model

1. The Initial Supervisory Meeting

This meeting would take place yearly and be approximately 1½ - 2 hours in duration. Both parties (supervisor and supervisee) should come to the table very well prepared.

This is not an informal meeting and should be treated seriously.

This meeting should be an in-depth discussion, reviewing the employee's progress, accomplishments, contribution, and work of the previous year. The employee should have some clear examples and indicators of success (e.g., completing a project, writing a report, negotiating a business opportunity, implementing a process or procedure, etc.). The supervisor should also come to the meeting with examples of the employee's productivity and accomplishments.

To provide an appropriate structure to this discussion, an agreed upon set of questions should be crafted ahead of time. (Later in this chapter, we will strongly suggest seven to consider.) These questions promote good dialogue, reveal areas of strength, and focus on areas of needed development. Creating these questions together enables both parties to "own" the process and, therefore, the outcomes.

The following questions are working examples that many people have found helpful and constructive. Both the supervisor and the supervisee must answer these questions before they meet for the initial meeting. The purpose of this is to ensure both parties are prepared for the meeting, and the homework enables each party to share their perspective with each other and promote a two-way dialogue.

1. When you look back over the past year, what stands out to you regarding what you have accomplished? Please be as specific as possible.

2. What have been some important "lessons learned" from the past year? This could be either positive or negative lessons (e.g., "I learned that I am a little too ambitious when I think about what I can

actually accomplish," "I am better at project management than I originally thought," or "I have to be more rigorous in establishing timelines and deadlines.")

3. What have been some challenges or difficulties you have encountered over the year? Have there been any disappointments?

4. What are some things you would like to accomplish over the next 6-12 months? (Please provide a rationale for each goal and a way to measure them.)

5. What are 1-2 areas of "needed development" you need to work on this year? Why do you need to work on them? How will they enhance your effectiveness (e.g., "I need to be more assertive in meetings"; "I need to become a more effective listener"; or "I need to focus my attention and energy on fewer things and not try and do everything")?

6. What support (e.g., education, specific courses, coaching, experiences, etc.) do you believe would be essential in helping you be successful this upcoming year? Please be specific.

7. How can I be supportive as your supervisor? (e.g., spend more time with you, develop a learning network, provide more timely feedback, etc.)

These questions create an information database that is rarely accessed in most supervisory meetings. It is obvious that if there is not a constructive and honest relationship based on trust between the two parties, these questions cannot be answered.

Both parties would share their perspectives and examples with each other. Reviewing one question at a time, they would identify common ground themes and clarify differences. This takes time, patience, and good listening.

The most important outcome or product of this meeting is an agreed upon set of performance goals for the employee. The employee needs to clearly understand what is expected of them over the next 3, 6 and 12 months; along with expected support, resources, lines of authority, reporting mechanisms, and ways to measure success and progress.

A brief follow-up meeting, 20-30 minutes or so, should be conducted about a week after the initial supervisory meeting. This time is an opportunity to have both parties reflect upon the review, share insights, right-size expectations, and correct any misconceptions.

2. Monthly Check-ins

These are brief, scheduled, "official" meetings (30 minutes) to maintain the dialogue, right-size expectations, provide feedback, problem solve, and build the supervisor-supervisee relationship. An employee should never be surprised at the end of the year that they are not meeting their goals and making a contribution. These monthly check-ins prevent this from happening. A short summary of this meeting should be recorded.

(Supervisors should also meet more frequently and informally with their direct reports during the month, to maintain good dialogue and oversight. The monthly check-ins are part of the "official" supervisory process.)

3. "Half-time" Check-in

This meeting would be conducted approximately six months after the initial meeting and be formal in nature. It should take about an hour and have some structure to it. This is an opportunity to determine what has been accomplished so far and what is reasonable to accomplish over the next six months. This "half-time" meeting could easily take an hour and, again, take some thought and preparation beforehand. (A brief review of the initial supervisory questions might be helpful.)

THE 360° FEEDBACK PROCESS

The 360° feedback process can provide additional information and insight that can inform the supervisory dialogue, and you can learn more about this process on pages 23-24.

However, note that the 360° process is a *learning process* and should never be used in a formal performance appraisal.

Ideally, it would be great if everyone throughout the organization participated in some kind of 360° process because of the self-awareness the process fosters and the opportunities it identifies for leadership and professional development. Realistically, the process should involve, at a minimum, all formal leaders in an organization.

---

4. A Learning Agenda

If a supervisory process is to have integrity and add value to the organization, it must include a learning process. After the yearly or initial discussion, both parties need to agree on a plan for improvement for the supervisee. Their improvement plan should focus on both the strengths and areas of needed development of the employee.

For example: If an employee realizes that they need help with managing their time, selected courses should be identified and participation ensured. Most importantly, the supervisor and supervisee need to agree on some practical measures to monitor the employee's progress regarding time management. Just taking the course is not enough, it must impact behavior (e.g., "We will monitor the number of times you deliver your monthly production reports on time" or "Periodically, we will keep track of your timeliness in our staff meetings"). The purpose is to measure results, not activities.

Another example: If an employee recognizes that they need to be more assertive in staff meetings because they often have something to contribute but don't. A learning agenda might involve taking some assertiveness training courses, reading appropriate books regarding assertiveness, and getting some counseling from a professional. The end result should be a change in the behavior of the employee, not more knowledge about assertiveness. The supervisee and supervisor can agree to track the number of times the supervisee speaks up in meetings.

Every employee should be working on their "learning agenda" throughout the year. There is always something to improve or build upon. Don't leave the supervisory meeting without agreeing upon your learning agenda with appropriate support (e.g., courses, coaching, reading, etc.).

The Rationale Behind the 7 Supervisory Questions

1. When you look back over the past year, what stands out to you regarding what you have accomplished? *(Please be specific.)*

The first question focuses on the positive accomplishments and successes of the employee. It creates the foundation for the Supervisory Dialogue and is the most important question in the entire process.

The positive beginning helps create a constructive context for the discussion by focusing initially on their contributions. It builds a helpful base for the discussion to follow.

2. What have been some important "lessons learned" from the past year?

This question assumes that the employee has actually learned some important things over the past year and asks the employee to reflect upon what they have learned.

These "lessons" can either be positive or negative. The team member chooses the direction here and the leader should make sure not all the lessons are on the negative side. For example:

- "I learned that I am a little too ambitious about what I can realistically accomplish - need to get reality checks before I commit to something."

- "I am a much better project manager than I originally thought. My group got all our major projects done on time this quarter."

- "I really have to work on my conflict resolution skills. I have avoided some important conversations that needed resolution."

- "My team is full of hardworking, dedicated people. I feel blessed to be their leader."

- "My people want to see me more often. I get caught managing the technical side of things and don't walk around and talk with folks."

- "We need to do a better job at boundary management with other teams and work groups throughout the division. As this initiative picks up more steam, we will be interacting with a lot of others."

3. What have been some challenges or difficulties you have encountered over the past year?

This question assumes there have been some "difficulties" and that it is helpful to identify them. This is not meant to be critical of the employee or put them on the defensive. It is meant to begin to discuss some of the sensitive issues that need to be addressed. The Supervisory Dialogue is a holistic approach to supervision and deals with the good as well as the not so great. Both are needed if the supervisory process is going to have real integrity.

By posing the question, the employee has the choice and freedom to acknowledge that everything hasn't been "perfect." It is important that the employee not dodge it by saying something vague like, "There were a couple of glitches last year but nothing worth talking about." They are soft selling their challenges. The team leader should be ready with their prepared examples to provide more rigor to the discussion. This question will be a diagnostic about how open and honest the team member really is about their shortcomings.

4. What are 1 – 2 areas of "needed development" you need to work on this year? *(How will you enhance your effectiveness?)*

This question begins to move into a sensitive area because the team member must be willing to admit they actually do have some things that need improvement. If there isn't a level of trust and a positive relationship present, the team member will be reluctant to share this.

This is another reason the team leader prepares their answers to the questions before the meeting. If the employee has some difficulty with this, the leader can then suggest some ideas and continue the dialogue.

We have found that most employees are all too willing to talk about their weaknesses and downplay their strengths. This is why you only ask for one or two areas of needed development, not seven or eight. If most people focus on improving one, possibly two areas, they will have done well.

What is important to pay attention to is how improving their areas of "needed development" will enhance their effectiveness as a team or group member. They must be clear about this, because they need to believe it is well worth the time and effort to improve. They must understand the tangible benefits for improving.

For example: "By learning the Critical Path Planning software program, I will improve my overall project management skills and keep my unit's work on track" or "By improving my decision making skills, I will be better prepared for the upcoming project we will undertake next month."

5. What are some things you would like to accomplish over the next 6 – 12 months? *(Please provide a rationale for each goal and a way to measure them.)*

It is important that the employee share what they believe they need to accomplish in order to contribute meaningfully to the team's goals. The fact that both parties have thought carefully about this question beforehand creates a "reality check" for the employee. If they go off on a tangent that really doesn't focus on the team's goals, the leader can provide some strong ideas about this.

It is important to have a rationale that is well thought out because the team leader can diagnose the effectiveness and strategic nature of the employee's thinking. The toughest element of this question is the *measurability* of the outcomes. Too often, individuals focus on activities (doing lots of things) rather than outcomes. For example:

- I will accurately complete the monthly audit report on time. (There is no "fuzziness" about this.)

- I will reduce the number of customer complaints in my unit by 30% in the first half of the year. (Note: They didn't go for a high number like 90%. The 30% figure seems doable.)

- I will reduce the office expenses (e.g. photo-copying, telephones, computers, electricity, etc.) by 15% by the end of the year.

- I will work with the Human Resources division and provide training in decision making for everyone in my unit. I will also work with H.R. to assess the effectiveness of my direct reports decision making skills throughout the year.

- I will spearhead Project X and successfully complete it on time and under budget.

6. What education/training do you think you will need to be successful this upcoming year? *(Please be specific.)*

At this stage, you have a great deal of helpful information regarding the learning and development needs of the employee. They will have discussed what they have learned, identified their areas of needed development, and their future goals. This information creates a **Learning Agenda** for the employee. This "agenda" should focus both on their strengths and areas of needed development.

The supervisor needs to solicit the employee's ideas about their educational and learning needs.

For example: If an employee realizes they need help managing their time, selected courses should be identified and participation ensured. Other examples might include: Visiting other departments on the campus to learn about best practices, choosing a mentor for advice and wise counsel, receiving coaching on a specific area of needed development, reading an article about a specific topic in order to continue building on a strength, attending a management/leadership program, writing a paper on lessons learned about a particular project, or taking an assertiveness course.

Every employee should have a "learning agenda" that they are working on throughout the next 6-12 months. Exceptional teams share their learning agenda with each other; this way everyone knows what others are working on. Having this information is helpful in several ways:

- It communicates that everyone is focusing on improving, which becomes a team norm.

- It can create the opportunity for team members to help each other. If one team member is strong in an area where another member needs help, a natural support network can be created.

- It creates a thoughtful risk taking opportunity for everyone. Sharing your agenda lets everyone know that you know what you need to work on. This shared risk tends to build a stronger team feeling.

7. How can I be supportive as your supervisor? (e.g., spend more time with you, provide access to outside resources, provide more timely feedback, etc.)

This question is important because it communicates to the employee that the leader is committed to their success and that they want to be supportive. It is essential that the leader probe a little with this question because employees might be reluctant to ask for help.

The leader can suggest ways they can be helpful:

- How would you like us to communicate over the next six months (e.g., face-to-face weekly meetings, a working lunch every month, a "walking meeting" weekly, etc.)?

- What should we agree to do if you encounter a problem or get stuck on a project? How can we be proactive when this happens (because it will happen)?

- Can you identify any organizational hurdles (e.g., politics, resources, connections, etc.) that might get in the way of successfully completing your goals? How can I be helpful with them?

- I can identify specific leaders you will need to talk with about the division's strategic planning process.

- There are faculty in the Business School that can help you with your strategic thinking about the retention rates of the division. I will put you in touch with them.

The key here is for the supervisor to commit to *specific* support and follow-through. This will help build the trust level and credibility of the relationship.

Summary

Obviously, these suggestions will take time and attention to be effective. All of it is do-able if the organization has the will and discipline to do it right. In the end, supervision is about developing the capacity of the people in the organization, creating a learning agenda so people can enhance their skills, and holding people accountable to agreed upon, meaningful goals.

ABOUT THE AUTHOR

Patrick Sanaghan
President
The Sanaghan Group

DR. SANAGHAN serves as the head of The Sanaghan Group, an organizational firm specializing in leadership development, executive coaching, strategic planning, and leadership transitions. Pat has worked with over 200 campuses and hundreds of organizations in the last twenty-five years. He has taught leadership to thousands of leaders in higher education, and helped over one hundred campuses conduct collaborative, transparent strategic planning processes. He is the co-author/author of six books, numerous articles, and several monographs in the fields of strategic planning, leadership, and change management. His most recent books include: Collaborative Leadership in Action and How to Actually Build an Exceptional Team. Dr. Sanaghan also serves as a board member of the College of Saint Benedict in St. Joseph, MN.

Made in the USA
Columbia, SC
01 June 2018